Year 6
Textbook

Published by Pearson Education Limited, 80 Strand, London, WC2R 0RL.
www.pearson.com/international-schools

Copies of official specifications for all Pearson Edexcel qualifications may be found on the website: https://qualifications.pearson.com

Text © Pearson Education Limited 2023
Produced by Just Content Ltd
Designed by PDQ Media Digital Media Solutions
Typeset by PDQ Media Digital Media Solutions
Picture research by Straive Ltd
Original illustrations © Pearson Education Limited 2023
Cover design © Pearson Education Limited 2023

The right of Lesley Butcher to be identified as the author of this work has been asserted by her in accordance with the Copyright, Designs and Patents Act 1988.

First published 2023

26 25 24
10 9 8 7

British Library Cataloguing in Publication Data
A catalogue record for this book is available from the British Library

ISBN 978 1 292 43327 1

Copyright notice
All rights reserved. No part of this publication may be reproduced in any form or by any means (including photocopying or storing it in any medium by electronic means and whether or not transiently or incidentally to some other use of this publication) without the written permission of the copyright owner, except in accordance with the provisions of the Copyright, Designs and Patents Act 1988 or under the terms of a licence issued by the Copyright Licensing Agency, 5th Floor, Shackleton House, 4 Battlebridge Lane, London, SE1 2HX (www.cla.co.uk). Applications for the copyright owner's written permission should be addressed to the publisher.

Printed in the UK by Bell & Bain

Contents

1. Micro-organisms 2
2. Plant life cycles 18
3. Heart, lungs and circulation 36
4. Reversible and irreversible change 54
5. Forces in air and water 78
6. Electricity: changing circuits 96
7. Revision 110

Welcome to Pearson International Primary Science!

This book is a key part of your journey to becoming a young scientist.

Let's take a look at some of the features.

Introduction
This introduces you to what the lesson is about.

Information
These are some of the important things you will learn in the lesson.

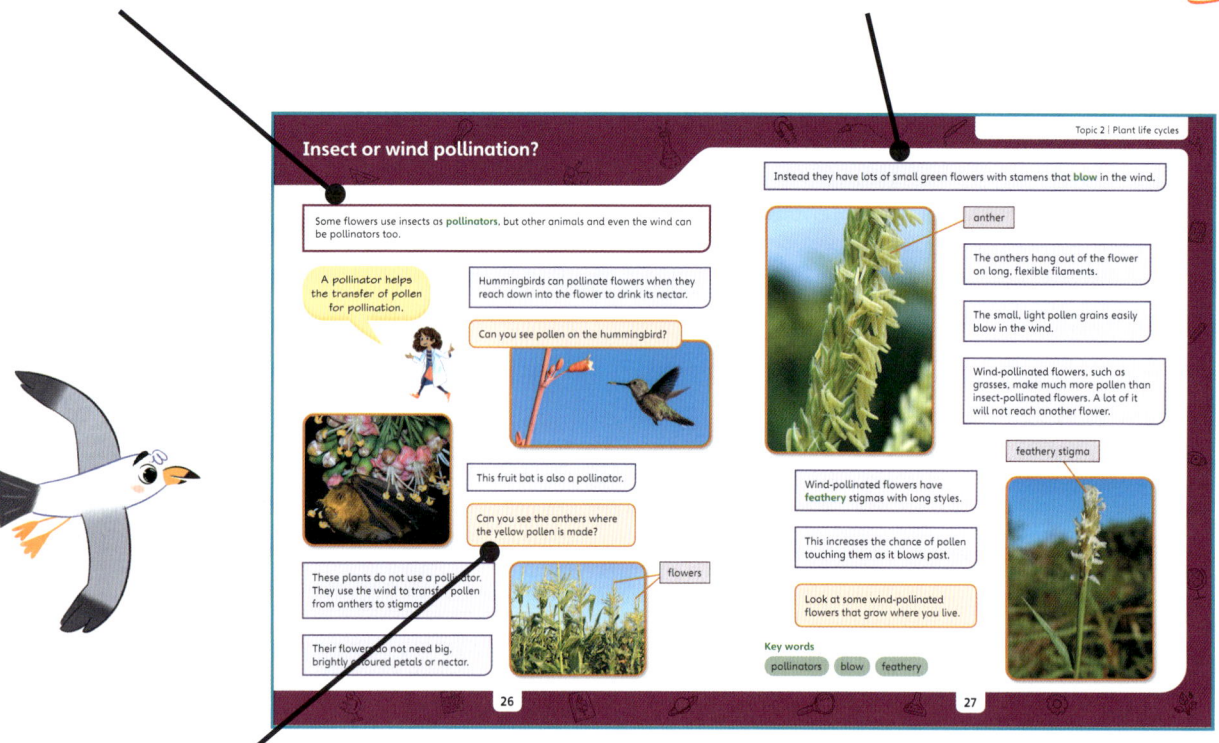

Questions
There are lots of questions within the lesson to challenge your thinking.

If you are very interested in science, the textbook shows you pictures of extra things to explore yourself.
After you have read these pages you could find out more about wind-pollinated flowers.

Key words
These are important words to know. They are highlighted in green in the lesson.

Mascots
These are helpful hints or questions from our mascots.

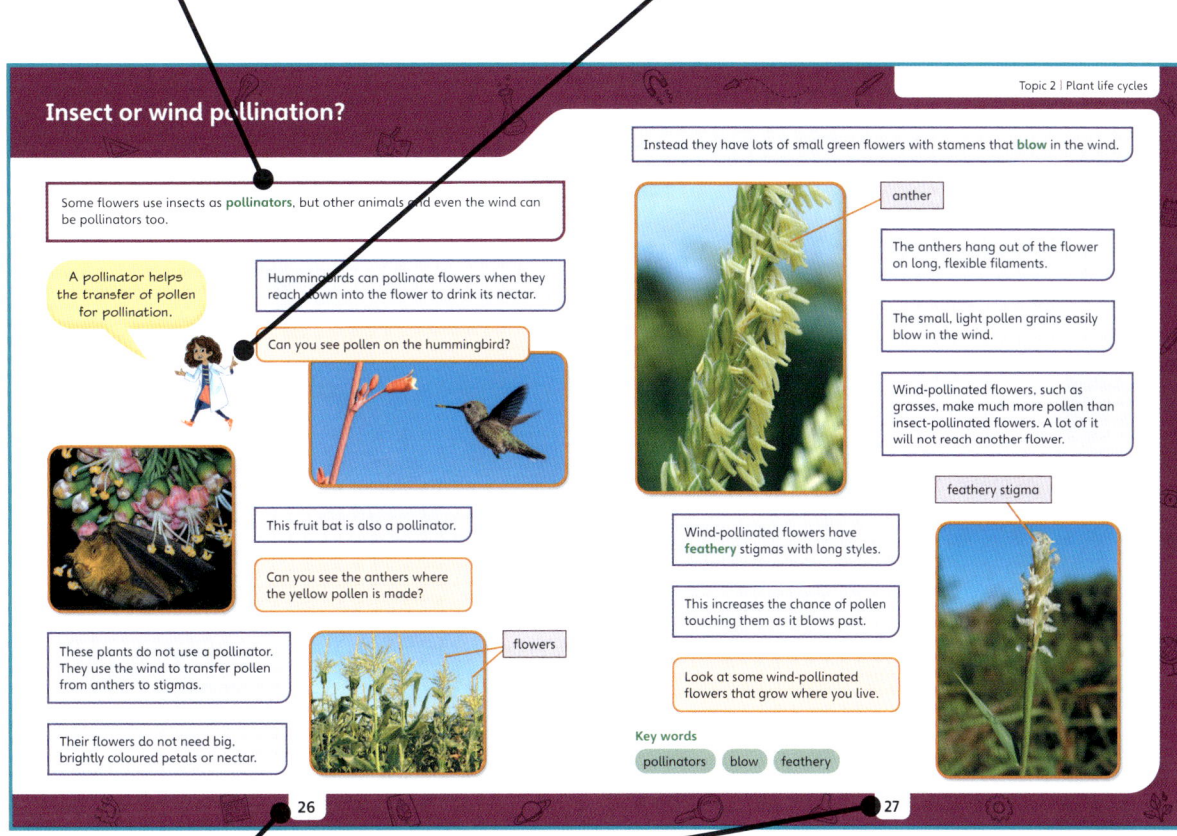

Page numbers
The page numbers for each lesson exactly match the page numbers in your workbook. This means you can easily find the workbook page for every textbook lesson.

You can use the textbook pages to help you with some of the workbook tasks. Sometimes the results table for an investigation is in the workbook.

Meet the mascots

Asha
This is Asha. She is good at science and helps others to **understand** things. Asha works **accurately** and will help you to do that too. She knows that many words in science have a very **precise** meaning and she points this out to you from time to time.

Marco
Meet Marco! He is **analytical**. He thinks carefully about how things in the world work. He likes **investigating** and tries to get reliable results by doing fair tests. Marco encourages you to **apply** your knowledge to work out answers whenever you can.

Victor the giant tortoise
Say hello to Victor. He is a giant tortoise from the Galapagos Islands. Victor is 120 years old! Victor is **observant** and keen to explore the world beyond his island. Victor is slow and **careful** but he plans his time well. He likes to **think** ... and what better place to do it than inside his shell!

Year 5 | Meet the mascots

Sully the gull
Wave hello to Sully. He is a type of bird called a gull. Gulls can be found all over the world! He is **curious**. Sully can fly up high or swoop down low to question things from different viewpoints. Sully knows that **asking questions** is the way that scientists start their own investigations.

Zorp the alien
This is Zorp! Zorp enjoys **exploring**. Zorp knows a lot about our Solar System and likes to share that knowledge. Zorp knows that lots of things on Earth are new to him, but he **discusses** them with friends and thinks of ways to find out things by himself too.

And finally ... you!
You are a very important part of these books. The books are here to tell you new things but also to help you to become a scientist. Scientists like to find out new things and to challenge their own ideas and those of others. We hope you enjoy exploring and investigating science, asking lots of questions and have fun!

Test and exam skills

Being prepared is the most important way to help yourself to do your best. Here are some ideas:

Planning ahead
- Write down the date of the test and count how many days you have to get ready for it.
- Divide up what you need to learn so that you will be ready BEFORE the test day. You are then less likely to worry that you do not have enough time.

Learning the topic(s)
It is not enough just to read about the topic. Do something ACTIVE such as:
- write down the important facts and the key vocabulary you must learn, not just everything that is in your textbook or workbook
- ask someone to test you by asking you some of the workbook questions
- write some sentences, missing out the key vocabulary. Take a photo of them if you can. See if you can complete the missing words in a few days' time. If you have a photo, you can easily do this more than once.

Know how to answer the questions in a test
- **Questions that ask you to tick, cross or circle your answer** often have instructions such as:

Put a cross (✗) in **one** box to indicate your answer.

Circle **two** animal groups this animal is in.

Put **one** tick (✓) in each row of the table to show something.

Check how many answers you are allowed to choose, then make your choice after looking at ALL the options. If you change your mind, make the change very clear.

- **Questions that have a short answer line and one mark**

  _____ (1)

  Write a one-word answer or a short phrase. The length of the answer line and the number of marks show you that this is what is needed here.

  e.g. Question: which part of a plant takes up minerals from the soil?

  Answer: **roots**

- **Questions that have one or two longer answer lines and one mark**

  _____

  _____ (1)

  Questions like this often ask you to describe something, define a word or answer a simple question. The length of the answer line and the number of marks show you this. Do not copy parts of the question in your answer.

  e.g. Question: What does the term _respiration_ mean?

  Answer: It is the **life process in which body organs use oxygen**.

- **Questions that have several answer lines, and more than one mark**

  _____

  _____

  _____ (2)

  Questions like this often ask you to explain something. The number of answer lines and the number of marks show you that you need to write something that contains two facts or ideas. Do not copy parts of the question in your answer.

  e.g. Question: Explain why a plant dies if it is left in a dark cupboard.

  Answer: Plant **leaves use light to make their food.** The plant in the cupboard **has no light so it cannot make any food.**

Notice that the answer does **not** start with 'A plant dies if it is left in a cupboard because ...'.

You will get **no** marks for writing this and it wastes time and answer space.

Write some questions of each type and give them to your partner to answer.

1 Micro-organisms

Micro-organisms are tiny living things. Let's look at some of the ways they are both useful and harmful to humans.

Micro-organisms are so small that we need a microscope to see them individually.

Bacteria are micro-organisms. We use some to make yoghurt and cheese, but other bacteria can harm us by causing food poisoning or disease.

Fungi can be large, such as mushrooms, but there are many microscopic fungi too. We use a microscopic fungus called yeast to make bread dough rise before baking it. Some microscopic fungi grow between our toes, or under our nails, causing unpleasant infections.

The picture shows some yoghurt that has been made using useful bacteria. It has not been covered or stored properly.

Can you see some blue and grey mould fungus growing on the top? It is feeding on the yoghurt and decaying it. We cannot eat food like this; it could make us ill.

Suggest a good place to store yoghurt.

What is a micro-organism?

Hundreds of years ago, people did not know that there were very **tiny** living things that they could not see.

Doctors did not know why **diseases** spread from person to person. Some thought bad air or bad smells caused diseases.

Many doctors in the 1600s wore clothes like these to take away bad smells.

The beak contained herbs and spices to keep smells away.

The stick made it easy to point at things so they did not have to touch anything.

They thought that if smells could not reach their body, they would not catch diseases from their patients.

Topic 1 | Micro-organisms

After a piece of equipment called a **microscope** was invented, scientists were able to find out more about very tiny living things.

one of the first microscopes

We call these tiny living things **micro-organisms**. They are so small that we need a microscope to see them.

A microscope **magnifies** things.

When tiny objects are magnified they look bigger and are easier to see.

Micro-organisms that cause diseases are sometimes called germs.
This is not a scientific word so we do not use it.

This is what microscopes look like today.

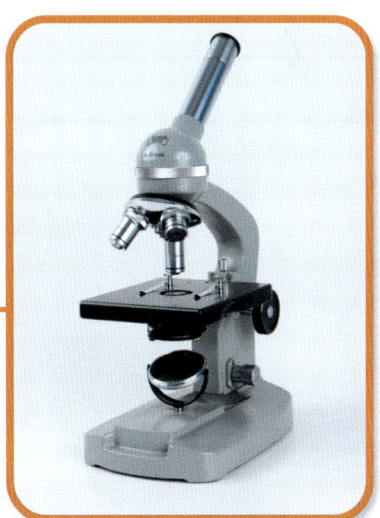

Many scientists have much larger microscopes than this. Their microscopes magnify objects more.

Key words

tiny   diseases   microscopes   magnifies   micro-organisms

5

Types of micro-organism

We have looked at many different animals and plants. There are many different types of micro-organism too. Some are useful to us, others are harmful.

We will look at three types of micro-organism in this topic:
- **viruses**
- **bacteria**
- **microscopic fungi**

All three types of micro-organism can make us ill.

Viruses

Viruses give us colds and influenza.

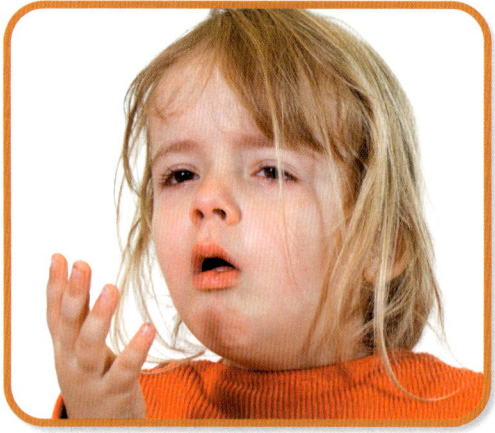

They also give us other diseases such as measles and chickenpox.

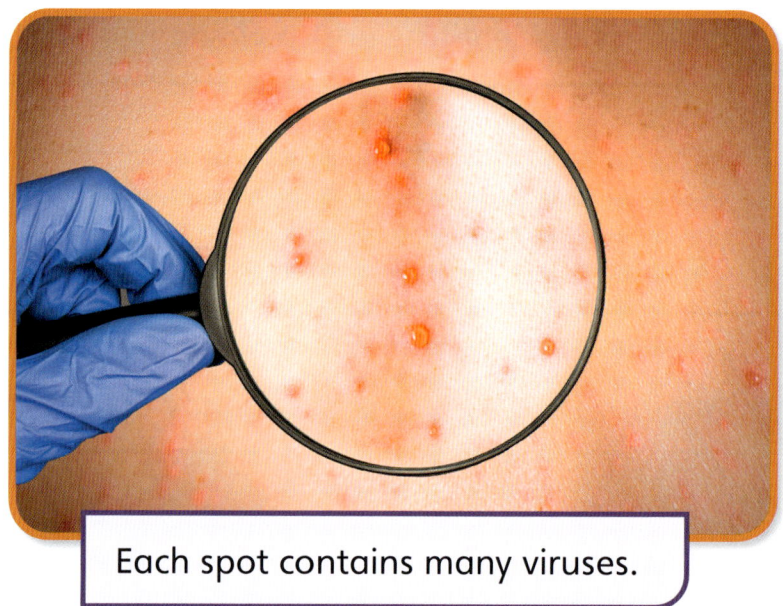

Each spot contains many viruses.

Topic 1 | Micro-organisms

Bacteria

Many bacteria live in our digestive system.
Some are harmful and may cause **food poisoning**, but some are useful.

Which part of the digestive system is shown by the cartoon figures?

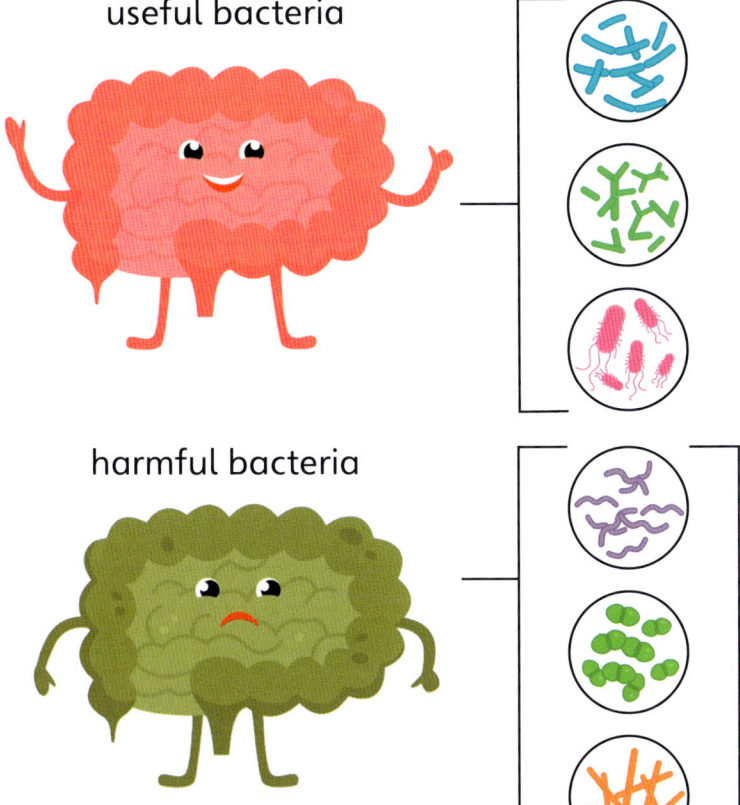

useful bacteria

- These bacteria are also found in yoghurt.
- These bacteria help to stop more harmful bacteria growing.
- Many types of *E.coli* like these help us to digest our food, but some types are harmful.

harmful bacteria

- Some of these bacteria cause food poisoning.
- They all cause illness and some are hard to kill.

Fungi

Only some fungi are micro-organisms.

This foot infection is caused by a microscopic fungus.

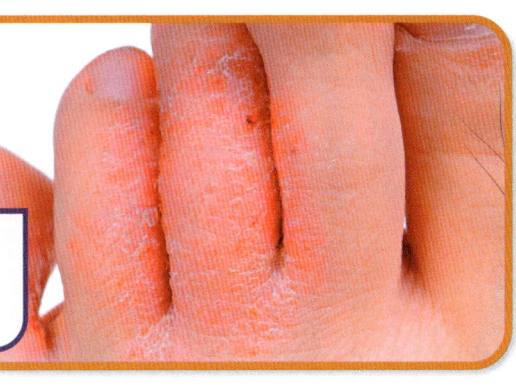

Key words

viruses   bacteria   microscopic   fungi   food poisoning

Food hygiene

Hygiene means doing things to stay **clean** and healthy. Food hygiene can prevent the spread of disease.

Washing hands

Our hands touch lots of things. We cannot see micro-organisms on the things we are touching.

Everyone who touches food should wash their hands with **soap** and water first. This helps to stop harmful micro-organisms going into the food.

Can you wash your hands for 20 seconds? Try it.

If micro-organisms are allowed to **grow** and **reproduce** on food, they may cause food poisoning.

Washing fruit and vegetables

Washing fruit and vegetables helps to remove the micro-organisms before we eat them.

Microscopic fungi are growing on this orange and have made it go **mouldy**.

Topic 1 | Micro-organisms

Storing food safely

Micro-organisms land on food from the air, from our hands and from insects. Insects bring micro-organisms from dead animals and bins onto our food.

If we **cover** food, it is harder for micro-organisms from insects to reach it.

What are the tongs for?

It is cool inside a **refrigerator**. Micro-organisms grow and reproduce more slowly here.

This is a kitchen where pasta is made.

Describe what the worker is **wearing** to help the pasta stay safe to eat.

Key words

hygiene   clean   soap

grow   reproduce   mouldy   cover   refrigerator   wearing

Mouldy bread

Moulds are types of microscopic fungi that live on food.

What makes **bread** go mouldy more quickly?

Let's do an investigation to find out.

Think of some questions you could ask about mouldy bread.

Does bread go mouldy more quickly in a warm place?

Have you seen mouldy bread?

Does bread need water to go mouldy?

Is mouldy bread nice to look at?

Which of these are **scientific** questions?

A scientific question is a question that can be answered by doing an investigation.

You will need:
- two slices of bread
- two transparent plastic bags that can be **sealed** closed
- some sticky labels.

Topic 1 | Micro-organisms

1. Decide on your scientific question.

2. a) What is the one thing you will change?
   b) What will you observe?

3. What must you keep the same?

4. Use one slice of bread in each bag. Make two labels to stick on each bag.
   a) Write what you are changing for each slice of bread on one label.
   b) Write 'do not open' on the other label.

5. Leave your slices of bread for one week. Look at them regularly, but do **not** open the bags.

Examples of labels:

cold place

DO NOT OPEN

warm place

There may be some harmful micro-organisms growing too.

Key words

moulds   bread   sealed

Useful micro-organisms

We have seen lots of ways that micro-organisms can harm our food, but they can also help us to make food.

Making bread

Yeast is a type of microscopic fungus. We use it to make bread **rise** before cooking it.

dough

time

The yeast feeds on sugar in the bread dough. It uses the sugar for **respiration**. This makes carbon dioxide gas. The bubbles of this gas make the dough rise.

bubbles of carbon dioxide

Mix some yeast, warm water and sugar together in a container.

Leave it in a warm place and watch this happen.

Topic 1 | Micro-organisms

Making yoghurt

Bacteria are used to thicken milk to make **yoghurt**.

First, the milk is heated to kill any harmful bacteria in it.

When the milk is cool, some specially **chosen** useful bacteria are added.

The useful bacteria change the milk as they feed on it, and grow and reproduce.

Making cheese

Cheese is also made using milk and specially chosen useful bacteria.

Some cheeses have a harmless, useful mould added to them too.

The blue parts of this cheese are a type of mould.

Can you see the line showing where the blue mould was put in?

Key words

yeast   rise   dough   respiration   yoghurt   chosen   cheese

13

Decay

When micro-organisms feed, they break down the materials they are feeding on. We call this **decay**.

These fruits are decaying.

Decay can be useful

Have you noticed that dead leaves or dead animals do not pile up for ever? They disappear because micro-organisms called **decomposers** feed on them.

Bacteria and microscopic fungi can both be decomposers.

When dead things decay, decomposers do not need all the **nutrients** in them. Some nutrients go into the soil.

Decomposers are an important part of all food chains. They help to **recycle** materials in dead plants and animals and their waste.

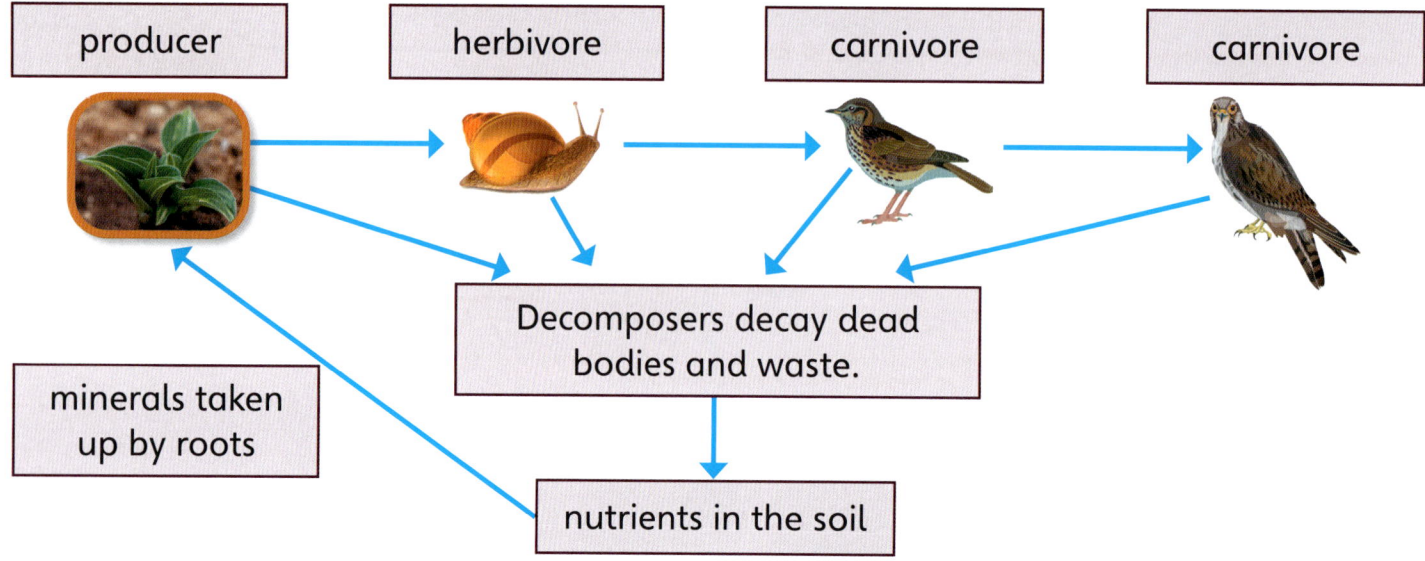

Topic 1 | Micro-organisms

Try making your own **compost** with your class or your family. You can use the compost you make to grow plants in.

Making compost

To make compost you need a container to hold the materials you want to decay.

Dead materials go in here.

Worms also help to make the compost.

A lid keeps the compost warmer and keeps animals out.

Compost is taken out here.

Decomposer micro-organisms need air. They need the **oxygen** in air for respiration. They get water from the dead materials you put in.

Decay happens faster in warmer places, so this will affect how soon your compost is ready to take out and use.

What to compost

vegetables

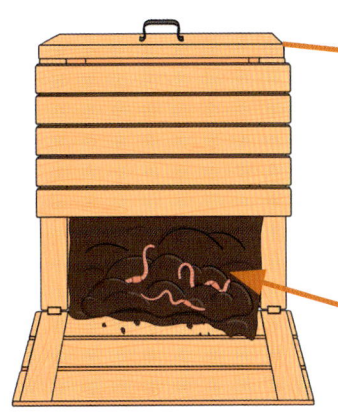
fruit

egg shells

coffee grounds and tea

paper scraps and bits of card

leaves, grass and dead plants

Key words

decay   decomposers   nutrients   recycle   compost   oxygen

End of topic questions

Micro-organisms

Read about Alexander Fleming, a scientist who made an important discovery using micro-organisms.

Professor Alexander Fleming lived from 1881 to 1955. The word professor is a title we give to very clever scientists who do investigations at universities or in hospital medical schools. The picture shows him working in his laboratory.

1 What equipment is he using?

He is working with micro-organisms so he is wearing a white laboratory coat that can be washed regularly.

2 What else should he wash regularly while working with micro-organisms?

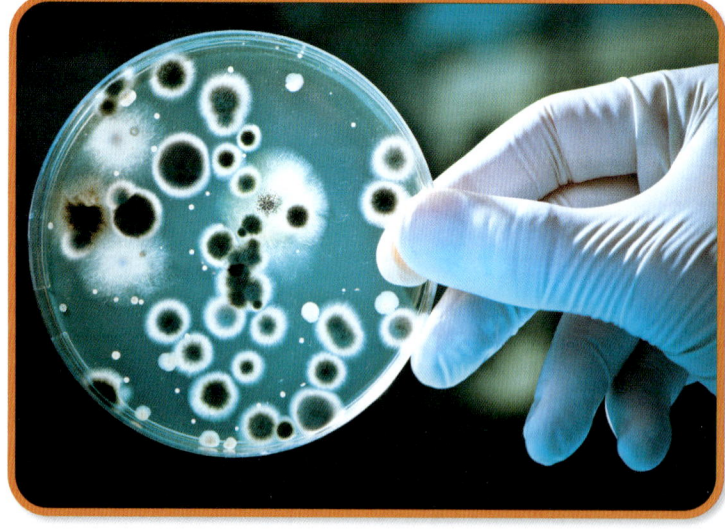

Professor Fleming was investigating micro-organisms by growing them on dishes like this one.

This picture shows a similar dish from a modern laboratory.

3 Can you see mould fungus growing in the dish?

The dish is called a Petri dish. It has jelly inside it that contains nutrients that micro-organisms can grow and feed on.

4 Suggest why Petri dish has a capital letter. Find out if you are correct.

Professor Fleming was growing bacteria in Petri dishes. One day he looked at this dish.

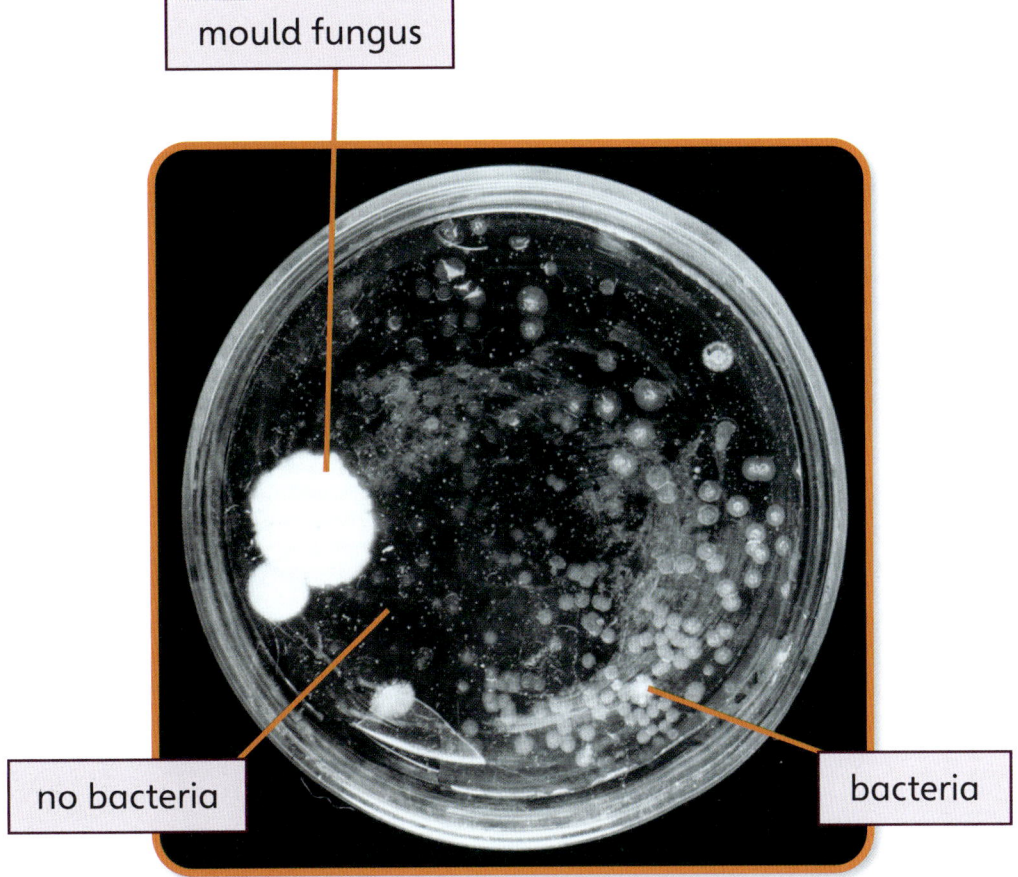

In places where there are very large numbers of bacteria, they look like small dots on the dish. Each dot may be many thousands of microscopic bacteria.

Professor Fleming was surprised to see that a mould fungus, called *Penicillium*, had also grown on the dish, but the bacteria were no longer growing beside it. They had all been killed.

Professor Fleming thought that the mould fungus must have made a chemical that killed the bacteria growing near it. We now know that the chemical this mould fungus made was penicillin.

Penicillin is a type of medicine, called an antibiotic, that doctors may prescribe today for some illnesses. Antibiotics only kill bacteria, not viruses.

5 Have you ever had any antibiotic medicine?

6 Find out about another famous scientist. Write about what they found out.

2 Plant life cycles

Some plants have flowers, which make seeds that grow into new plants. Let's look at how they do this.

Plants have flowers so that they can make seeds. This is how they reproduce. To make a seed the flower must move its pollen. It needs insects, other animals or the wind to do this.

Many flowers are brightly coloured to attract insects and other pollinators, such as hummingbirds, to visit them.

The picture shows a bee visiting a flower to collect pollen.

Look at the bee's leg. Can you see a big yellow pile of pollen it has collected?

Parts of a flower

Plants have flowers for the life process of reproduction. Flowers produce seeds and seeds grow into new plants.

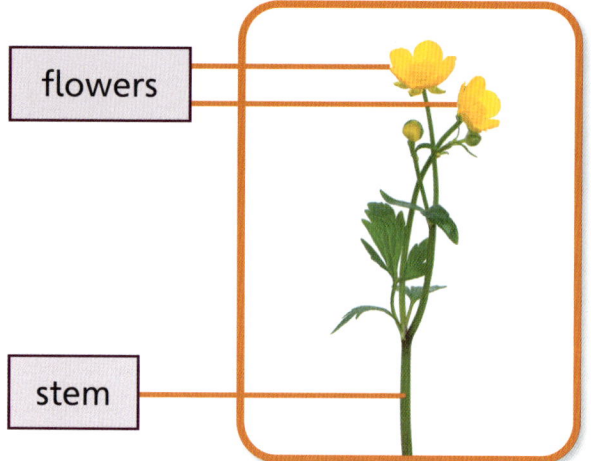

flowers

stem

This buttercup flower has five yellow **petals**. The function of the petals is to attract insects to the flower.

These bees have come to this flower to collect **pollen** for food.

This bee is covered in pollen. Can you see where it has come from?

Where do you think the bee will go next?

Before we find out where the bee goes next, let's look at the parts of a flower in more detail.

Topic 2 | Plant life cycles

This is a diagram of the parts of a flower. It is drawn like the scientific diagrams you saw of a beaker and a measuring cylinder.

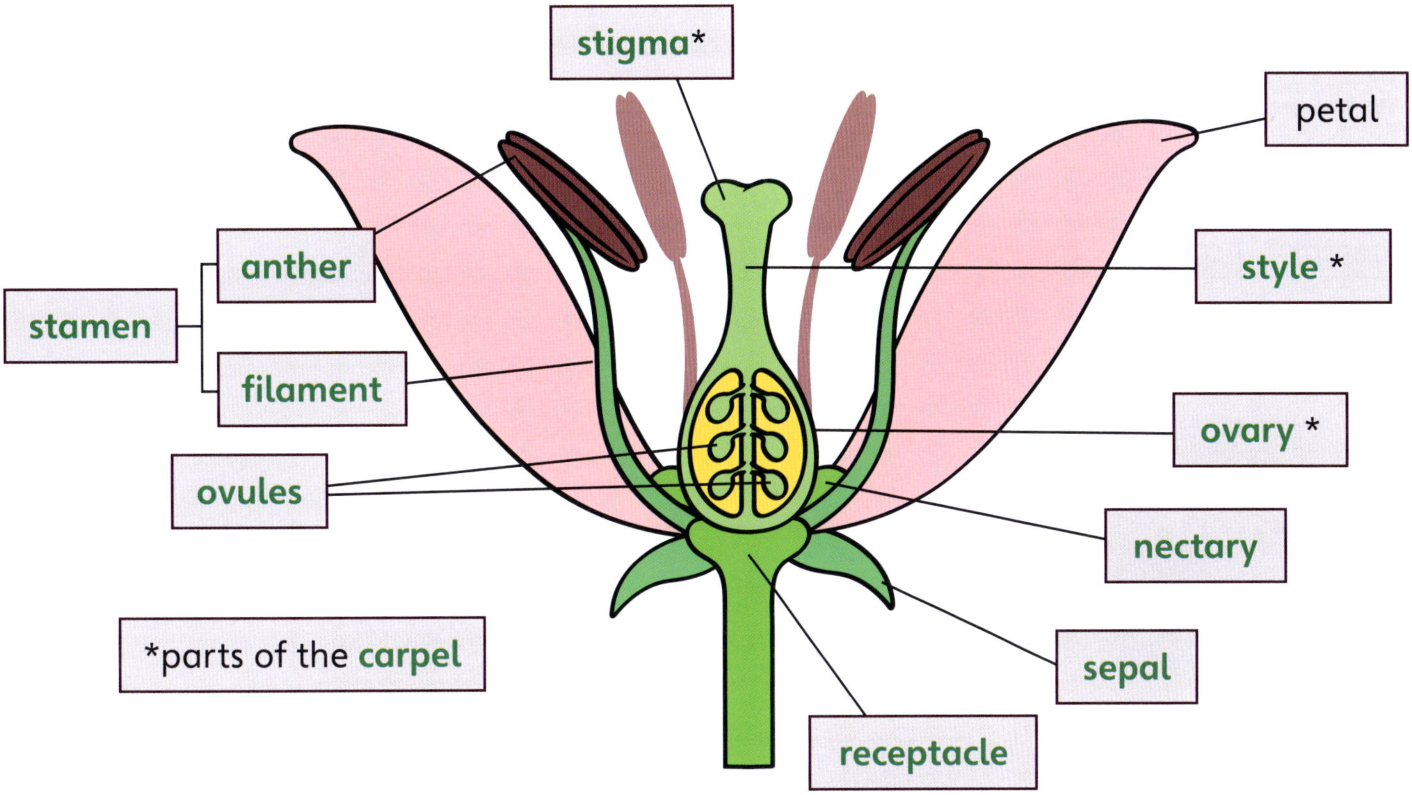

- stigma*
- petal
- stamen
  - anther
  - filament
- style *
- ovules
- ovary *
- nectary
- *parts of the carpel
- sepal
- receptacle

This is a photograph of part of a lily flower.

Can you see the two parts of the stamen?
Can you see the stigma and style?
Can you see pollen?

Key words

petals   pollen   stigma   style   ovary   nectary

sepal   receptacle   carpel   ovules   stamen   anther   filament

21

Functions of parts of a flower

Each part of a flower has a specific function.

sepals	protect the flower bud until it opens
petals	large and brightly coloured to attract insects
nectary	contains a **sugary** liquid called **nectar** to attract insects

This butterfly is drinking nectar.

Can you see its uncurled mouthparts?

Pollen sticks to insects that enter the flower to eat or drink.

Stamens are the male parts of a flower. Each stamen has two parts.

anther	makes pollen, which is needed for **pollination**
filament	holds the anther up and bends to help brush pollen against insects

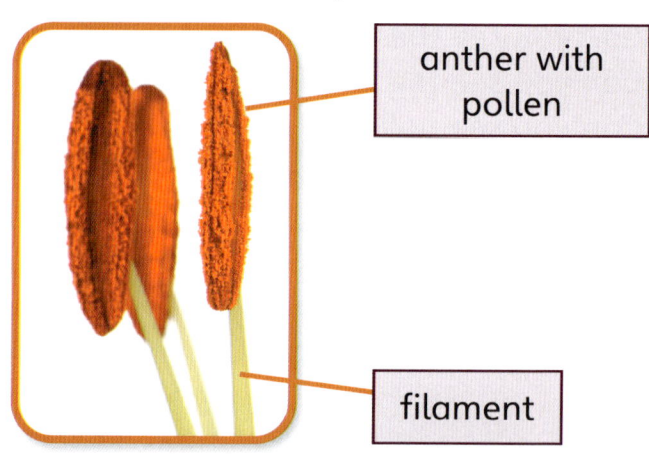

anther with pollen

filament

22

Topic 2 | Plant life cycles

Carpels are the female parts of the flower. Each part of a carpel has a different function.

stigma	has a **sticky** surface for pollen to land on
style	holds the stigma up and connects it to the ovary
ovary	the wider part of the carpel containing the ovules, the ovary will later become a **fruit**
ovules	these will later become **seeds**

Carpels are often in the centre of a flower like this one.

Can you see six stamens in a circle around the carpel?

The wider top part is the stigma.

The bright yellow colour attracts insects to go deep into the flower.

All the parts of the flower are joined to the receptacle.

Now find some of these parts on flowers that grow where you live.

Key words

sugary   nectar   pollination   sticky   fruit   seeds

23

Pollination and fertilisation

When insects enter a flower, they are dusted with pollen from the anthers.

You saw this bee on page 20. When this bee goes to another flower, some of the pollen on its body may fall off.

Pollen may land on the stigma of the same flower or another flower. This is pollination.

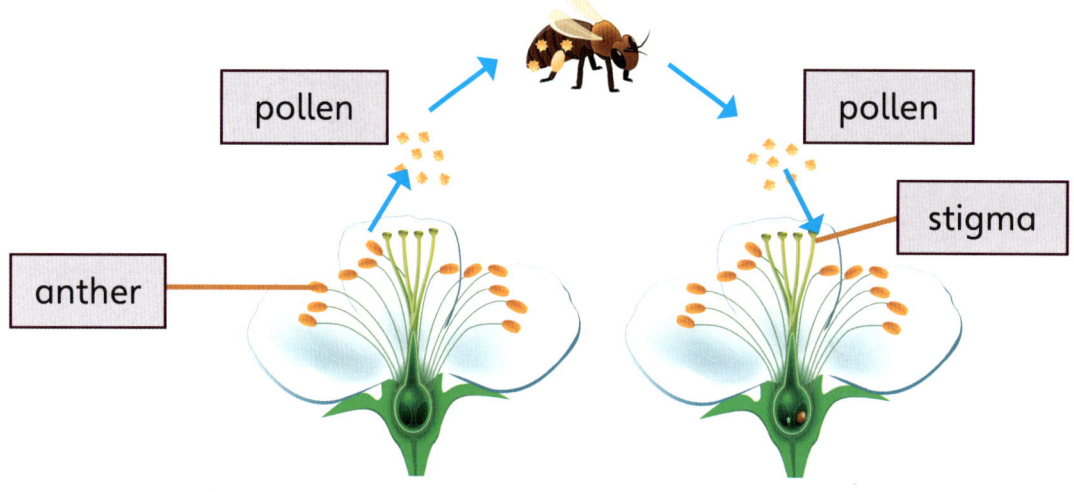

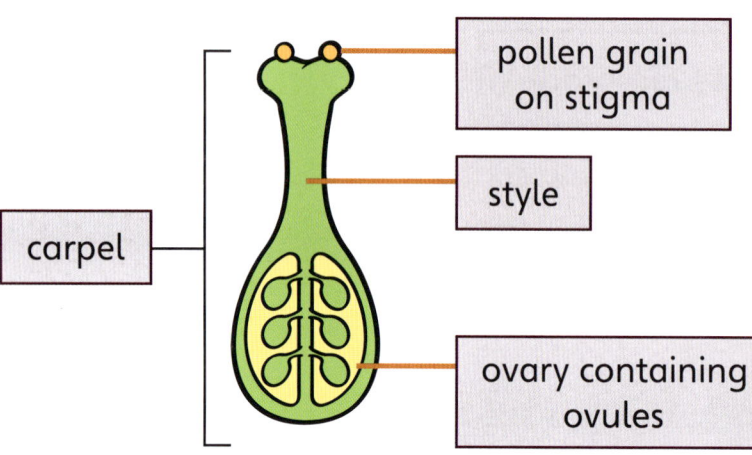

Pollination is the **transfer** of pollen from the anther to the stigma of the same flower or a different flower.

Together, the stigma, style and ovary containing ovules are called a carpel.

The pollen grain contains **half** the **information** to make a seed. It is inside the pollen grain in a **nucleus**.

Each ovule also contains a nucleus with the other half of the information.

The pollen grain sends its half of the information down to an ovule. It grows a **pollen tube** through the style to get it there.

Can you see another pollen tube starting to grow?

Where do you think it will go?

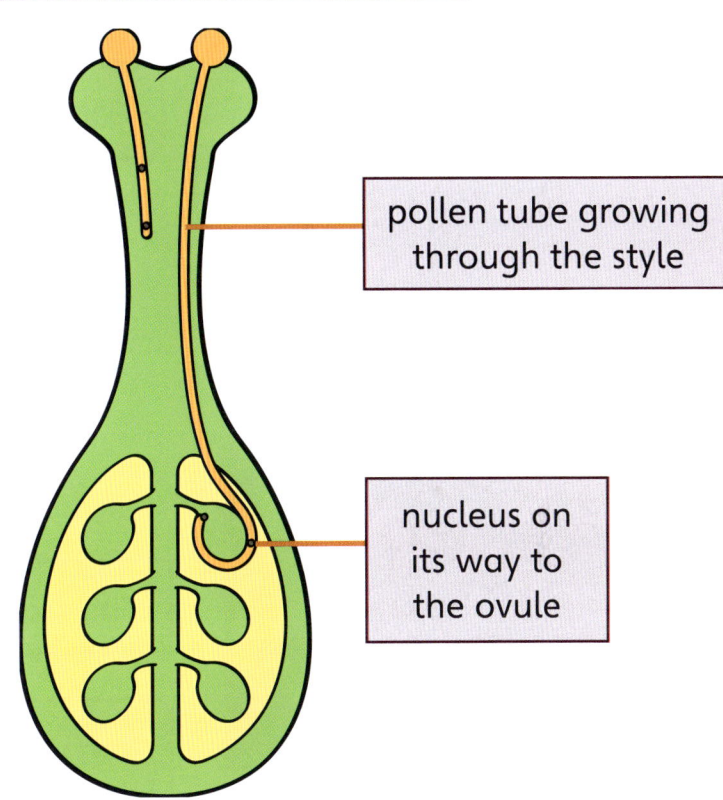

pollen tube growing through the style

nucleus on its way to the ovule

Fertilisation is when a nucleus from the male pollen grain **joins** with a nucleus in the female ovule inside the ovary.

After fertilisation, each ovule becomes a seed.

Key words

transfer · half · information · nucleus · pollen tube · fertilisation · joins

Insect or wind pollination?

Some flowers use insects as **pollinators**, but other animals and even the wind can be pollinators too.

A pollinator helps the transfer of pollen for pollination.

Hummingbirds can pollinate flowers when they reach down into the flower to drink its nectar.

Can you see pollen on the hummingbird?

This fruit bat is also a pollinator.

Can you see the anthers where the yellow pollen is made?

These plants do not use a pollinator. They use the wind to transfer pollen from anthers to stigmas.

Their flowers do not need big, brightly coloured petals or nectar.

flowers

Instead they have lots of small green flowers with stamens that **blow** in the wind.

anther

The anthers hang out of the flower on long, flexible filaments.

The small, light pollen grains easily blow in the wind.

Wind-pollinated flowers, such as grasses, make much more pollen than insect-pollinated flowers. A lot of it will not reach another flower.

Wind-pollinated flowers have **feathery** stigmas with long styles.

This increases the chance of pollen touching them as it blows past.

Look at some wind-pollinated flowers that grow where you live.

feathery stigma

Key words

pollinators   blow   feathery

Seeds

Each fertilised ovule becomes a seed. The diagram shows a flower from a tomato plant and a tomato.

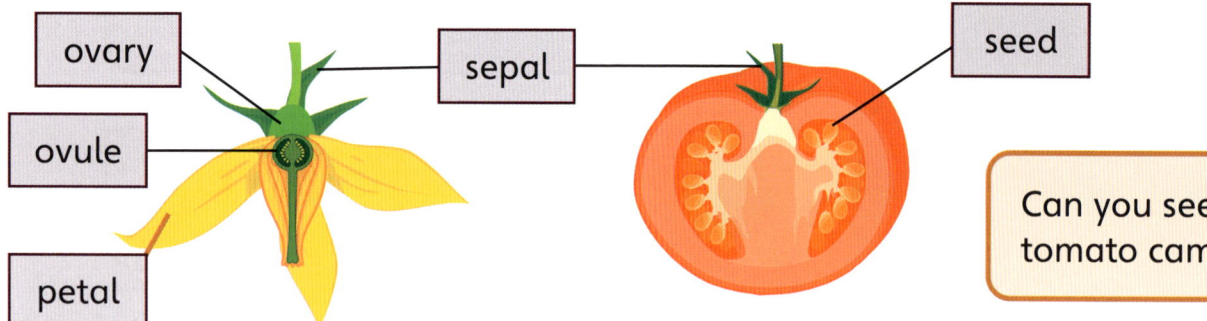

ovary | sepal | seed
ovule
petal

Can you see where the tomato came from?

In the wild, seeds need to be spread out or **dispersed**.

Dispersed means spread out over a wide area.

This is so that new plants do not have to compete with the parent plant for water, minerals or light.

Some ways that seeds can be dispersed are shown on these pages.

Discuss with a partner. Which have you seen?

These sycamore seeds twist and blow in the wind.

wind

Can you see the **dandelion** seeds? They are blown by the wind.

wind

Topic 2 | Plant life cycles

animals

This has **hooks** that stick to the fur of animals.

animals

Animals pick up seeds and **nuts** to eat. They drop some on the way home.

animals

There are seeds inside the **berries** and other fruits that birds eat. The seeds are not digested so they reach new places when egested.

explosion

This seed pod dries and splits open, flicking the seeds out.

wind

The **poppy** seed pod dries out too. The wind shakes the seeds out.

water

Coconuts are dispersed long distances by water.

Lotus flowers disperse seeds in water too. Find a picture of this.

Key words

dispersed   dandelion   hooks   nuts   berries   poppy   coconuts

Seed germination

After dispersal, seeds start to grow into new plants.

Some seeds need to be warm, others colder. Some may need light or dark conditions to start their growth. For many seeds, these factors do not matter.

But all seeds need water and oxygen from the air to start to **germinate**.

They need water to help the seed split open and also to help it digest its food store. Seeds need oxygen for respiration to be able to use the food store to grow.

food store inside seed

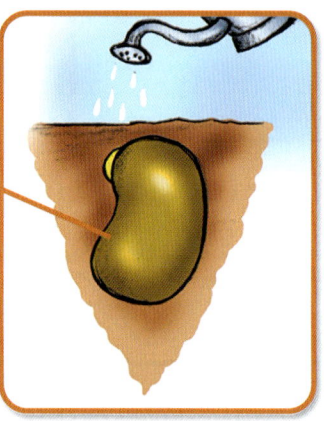

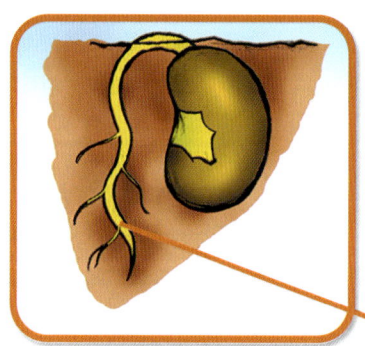

When the young plant has a root, it can take in its own water and minerals.

A root grows first.

Leaves can make food for the plant.

Now the young plant has used up its food store, but it has leaves. Now it needs sunlight to make its own food.

Plan an investigation to show that seeds need water and air to germinate.

1. Write a scientific question.

2. Use three groups of seeds so that some have:
   - water **and** air
   - water but no air
   - air but no water.

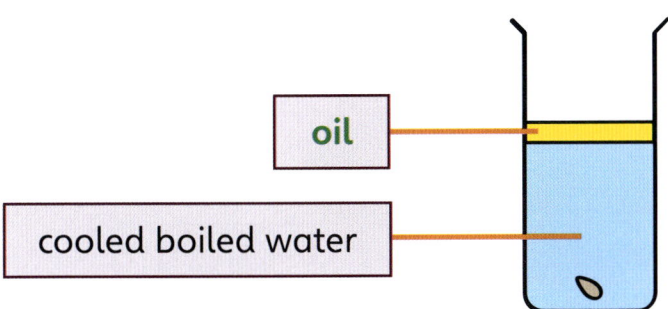

You can stop your seeds getting air by using cooled, boiled water and a layer of oil.

3. Think about what must stay the same.

4. Decide what equipment you will need. What will the seeds grow in?

Key words

germinate   oil

The life cycle of a flowering plant

Flowering plants are plants that have flowers to reproduce.

Not all plants have flowers. Some have cones.

a tree with cones

These plants do not have flowers or cones.

fern

moss

You have met the idea of a **life cycle** before.

Yes, when a frog's egg hatched into a tadpole it grew into an adult frog that lays eggs.

When seeds start to grow we say they are germinating. They grow into plants that have flowers. The flowers are pollinated, then the ovules are fertilised and the seeds that are made are dispersed.

Topic 2 | Plant life cycles

The life cycle of a flowering plant

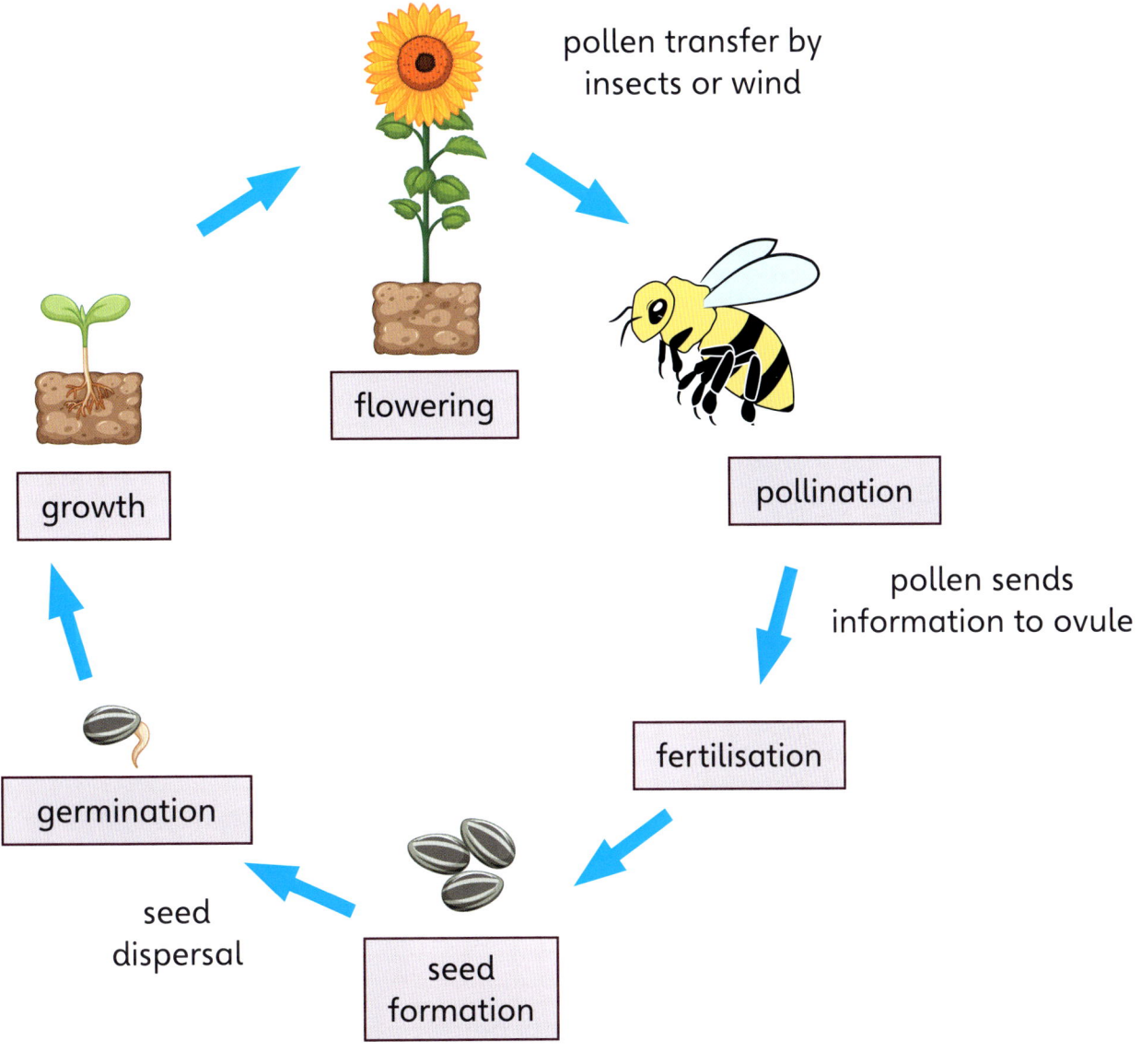

The stages of a life cycle must happen in the same order each time. If one stage does not happen, the cycle stops. If the plant's flowers are eaten, it cannot make seeds.

Bees are very important pollinators.

Predict what may happen if we do not help bees to survive.

Key words

life cycle

End of topic questions

Plant life cycles

1 Discuss these pictures with a partner.
- Identify as many parts of each flower as you can.
- Predict whether each flower is insect-pollinated or wind-pollinated. Give a reason for your choice.

What is protecting the flower that is still a bud?

Can you see anthers and filaments here?

Some flowers have sepals that are very similar to their petals.

Topic 2 | End of topic questions

Can you see stamens?

Can you see a stigma?

Can you see pollen on some of the petals?

What colour are the stigmas on this grass?

These flowers are on a fruit tree.

What happens after these flowers have been pollinated?

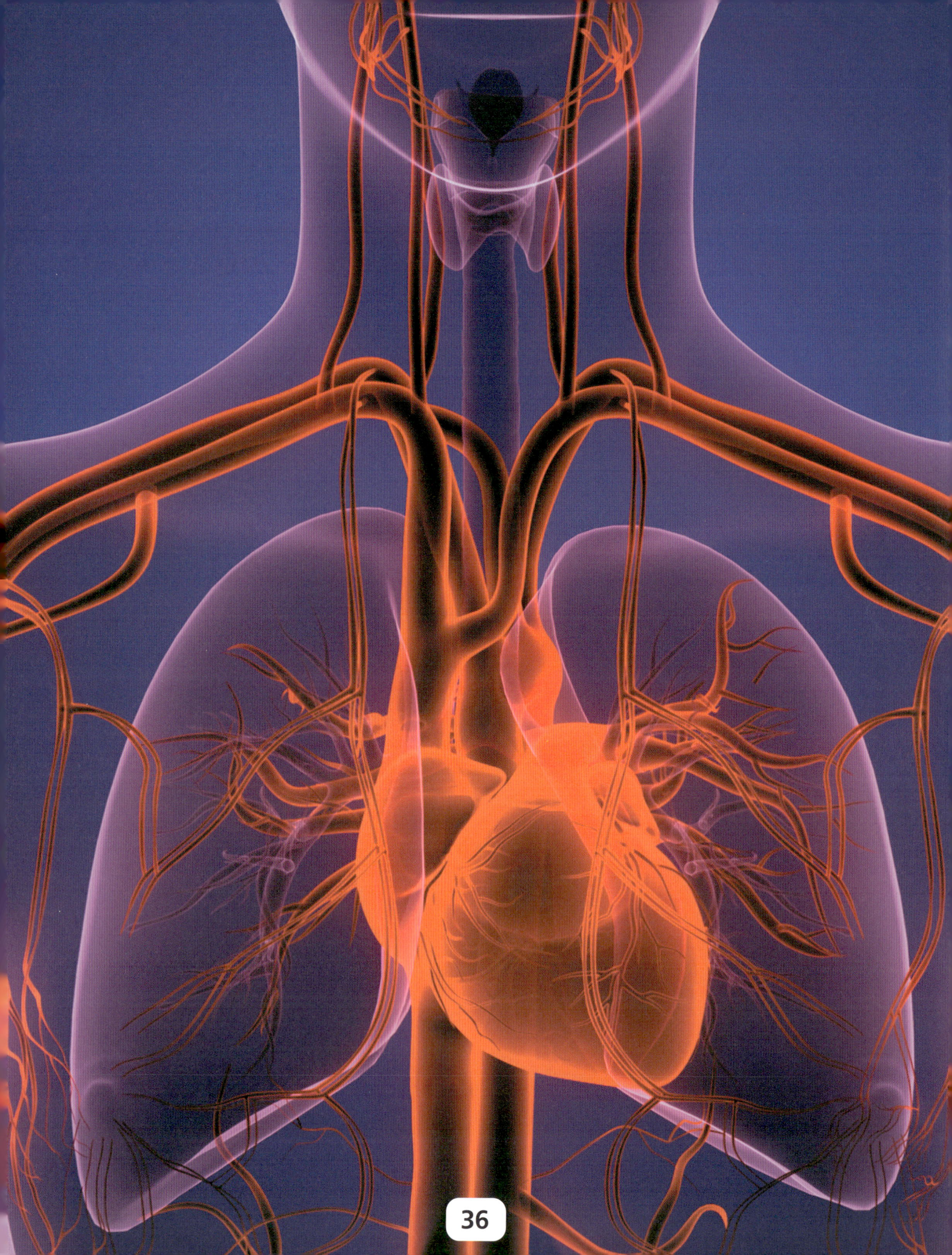

3 Heart, lungs and circulation

Our heart and lungs work all the time to keep us alive. Let's look at what they do.

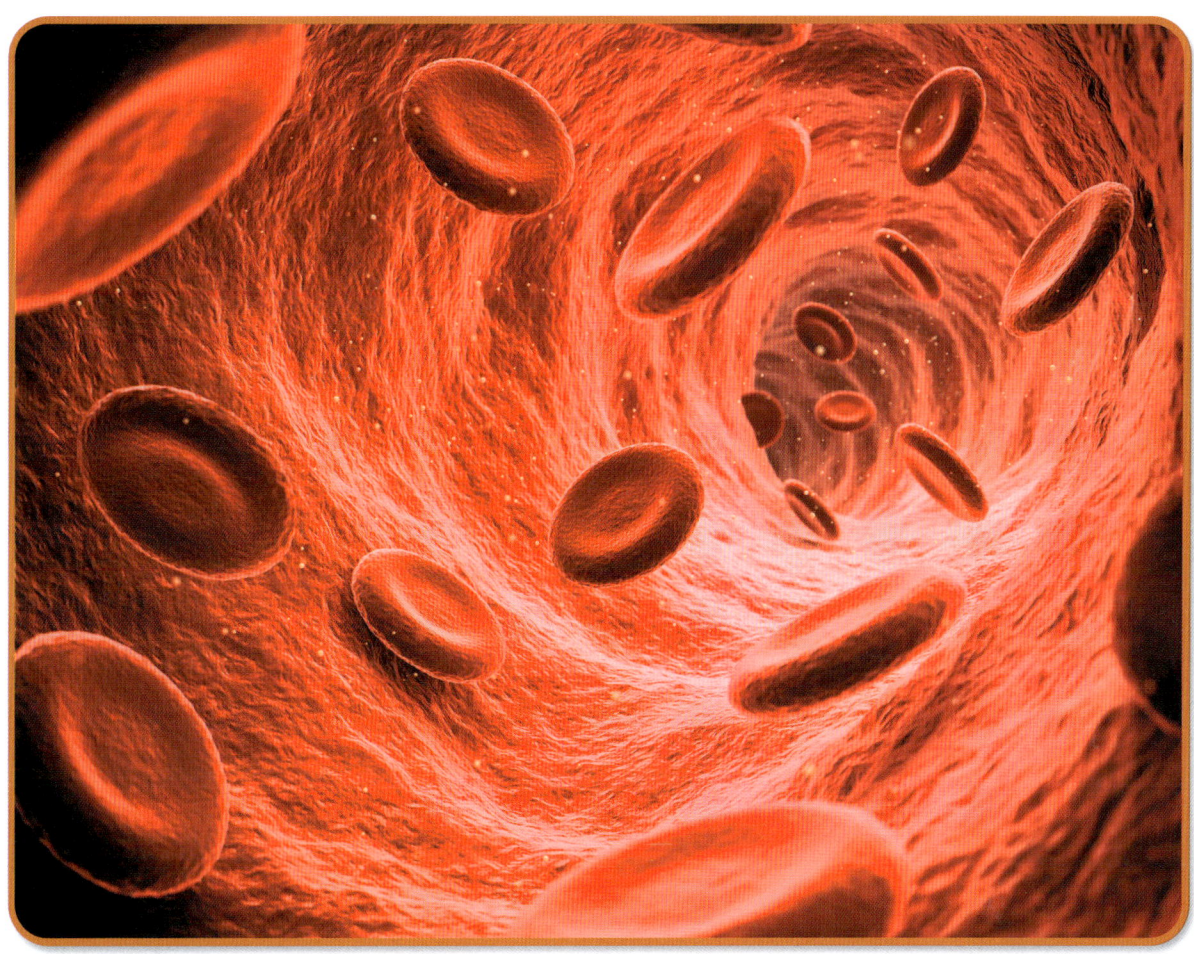

Our heart and lungs are organs. Our body has many other organs, such as the stomach and the brain. They all need oxygen and nutrients to work because they are used for respiration.

Our lungs take air in and out of our bodies. We call this breathing. Our blood takes the oxygen to all parts of our body in blood vessels. The heart pumps all day and all night to keep the blood moving in them.

Look at the picture.

Imagine you are going on a journey through this blood vessel. What can you see? Where will you go? The big discs you can see are red blood cells carrying the oxygen. In real life you need a microscope to see them. Do you remember where blood cells are made?

The circulatory system

The body is made up of different systems.

In Year 5 you learned about the digestive system. The stomach is one of the many parts that all work together to digest food.

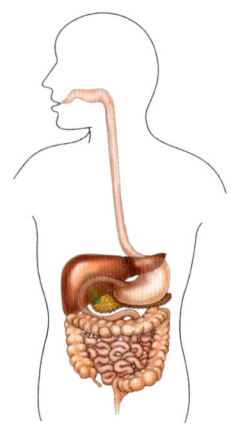

Find the stomach on the diagram.

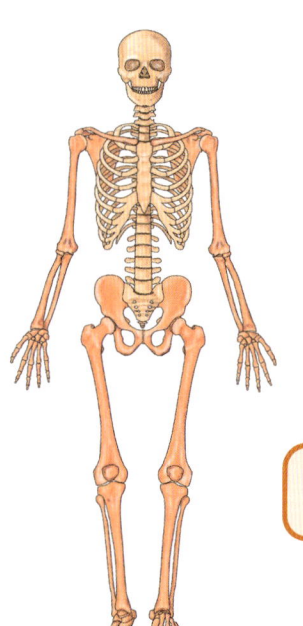

Before that, you looked at the skeletal system. It is made up of many bones.

Some of the bones protect organs like the **heart**, **lungs** and brain.

Find the rib cage on the diagram.

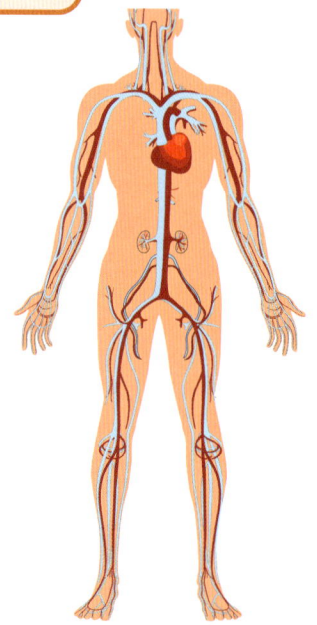

The heart and the **blood vessels** that carry blood around our body make up the circulatory system.

Look at the arms, legs and head. Blood vessels shown in red take blood to these places. Blood vessels shown in blue take the blood back from them to the heart.

Topic 3 | Heart, lungs and circulation

Our heart is made of a special type of muscle that is only found in the heart.

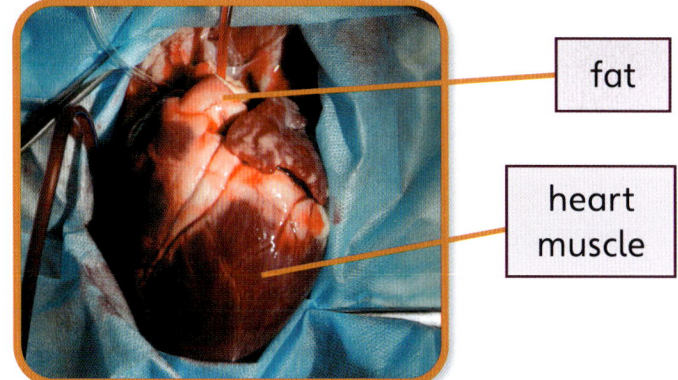

fat

heart muscle

The function of the heart is to **pump** blood around the circulatory system. To do this it **contracts** and then **relaxes**, just like our other muscles.

But the special thing about heart muscle is that it never stops for a rest.

When your leg muscles are **tired**, you can stop for a rest.

Each time the heart muscle contracts, it pumps blood to the lungs and around the rest of the body.

Hold something you can squeeze, such as a soft ball, to model the pumping action of the heart.

Do about one squeeze every second.

How soon did your hand muscles get tired of pumping?

Key words

heart   lungs   blood vessels   pump   contracts   relaxes   tired

What does the heart do?

The heart pumps blood to the lungs and around our body.

Blood vessels going to and from the heart contain blood.

Blood is a mixture. Most of it is water. The red **blood cells** in blood give it a red colour.

As well as oxygen, blood takes water and nutrients to all parts of our body.

The nutrients come from digested food that was absorbed in the small intestine.

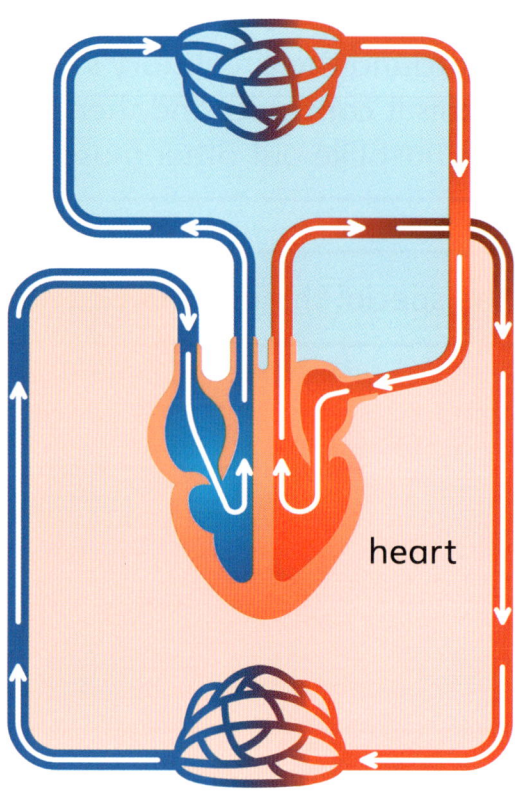

inside lungs

heart

all parts of the body

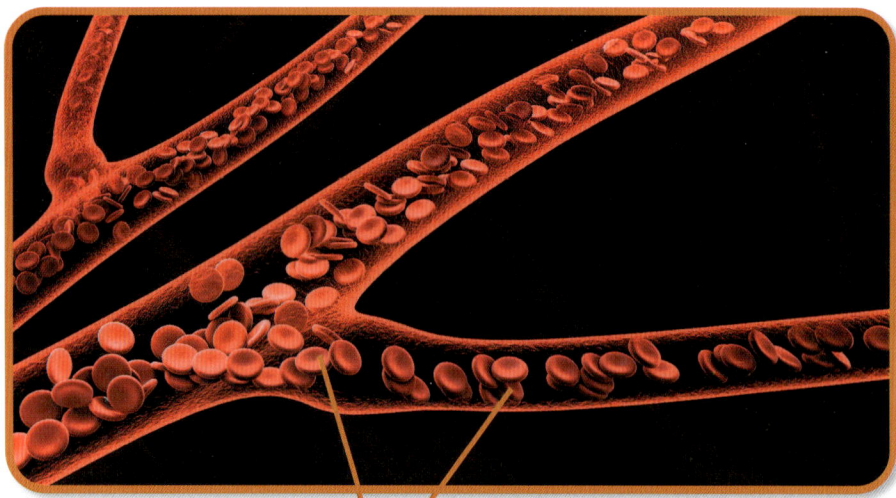

Blood cells carry oxygen to muscles.

Blood vessels are like long tubes. The liquid blood is inside them.

Can you remember where blood cells are made?

Topic 3 | Heart, lungs and circulation

Can you see any blood vessels in your wrist? Or the back of your hand?

The ones you can see are called **veins**. They are carrying blood from your hands back to the heart.

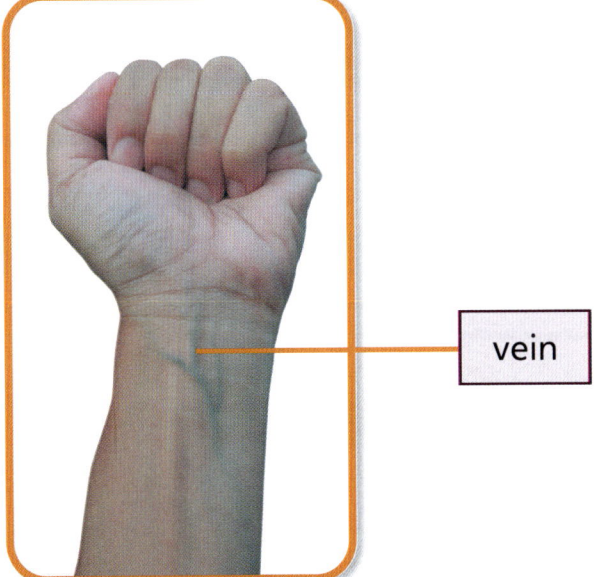

vein

Place the tips of your first two fingers onto the wrist of your other hand.

Place your fingers gently here on this blood vessel.

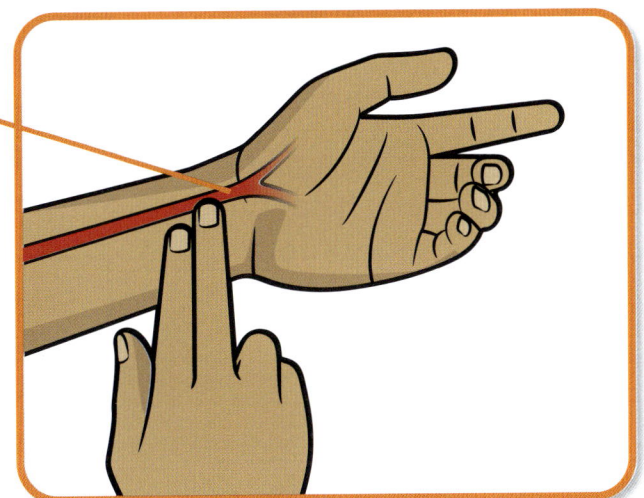

Can you feel a **pulse** of blood? This is your radial pulse.

The blood vessel you are feeling now is an **artery**. It is bringing blood to your hand. The veins you looked at earlier will take blood from your hand to your heart.

The pulse of blood is at the same speed as your heart is contracting.

Key words

blood cells   veins   pulse   artery

Investigating pulse rate

Your heart rate is the number of times your heart contracts in one minute. We sometimes see this written with the unit of beats per minute.

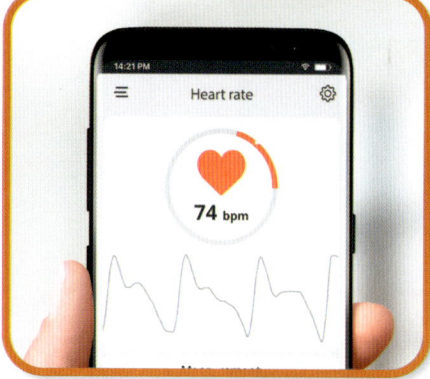

What is this person's heart rate?

On the screen the unit is shortened to bpm.

Measuring **pulse rate** is an easy way of measuring heart rate. Let's investigate how pulse rate changes when we **exercise**.

Scientific question: How does exercise **affect** pulse rate?

Work with a partner's help, but you can both investigate your own pulse rate. You will need:
- a stopwatch
- a skipping rope or a step.

1. Sit down. Sit still for a minute or two before starting. Find your radial pulse (see page 41). If you cannot find it, try to find the pulse in your neck.

2. Ask your partner to time 20 seconds. Count your pulse rate while you are sitting. Multiply it by 3 to change it to beats per minute. This is your **resting pulse rate**.

Topic 3 | Heart, lungs and circulation

3. Stay seated and repeat step 2 two more times. This gives you a more **reliable** resting pulse rate. Calculate an **average** (mean) if you can.

4. Stand up. Stay standing up for a minute before starting. Now take three measurements of your standing pulse rate.

5. Sit down and plan some exercise that you can count. For example, you could skip 20 times or step on and off a step 20 times. Start exercising when your pulse rate is back to its resting rate.

6. Count out loud as you exercise, so your partner will know when you finish. As soon as you finish, your partner will start timing 20 seconds. Count your pulse rate **immediately** after you stop exercising.

7. Sit down and wait a few minutes for your pulse rate to go back to your resting pulse rate. Your partner can do their own counting during this time.

8. Repeat the same exercise two more times, with two more pulse counts and rests.

9. Look at your results. How does exercise affect pulse rate?

When you stand, your heart has to work a bit harder to **circulate** blood around your body. When you exercise, your heart works even harder, so it contracts faster. During exercise, your muscles need more oxygen and nutrients for respiration, so they can keep contracting too.

Key words

pulse rate · exercise · affect · resting pulse rate · reliable · average

The respiratory system

The lungs are located in the **thorax**.

nose and mouth

trachea

right lung

left lung

Your left lung is on the same side of your body as your left hand!

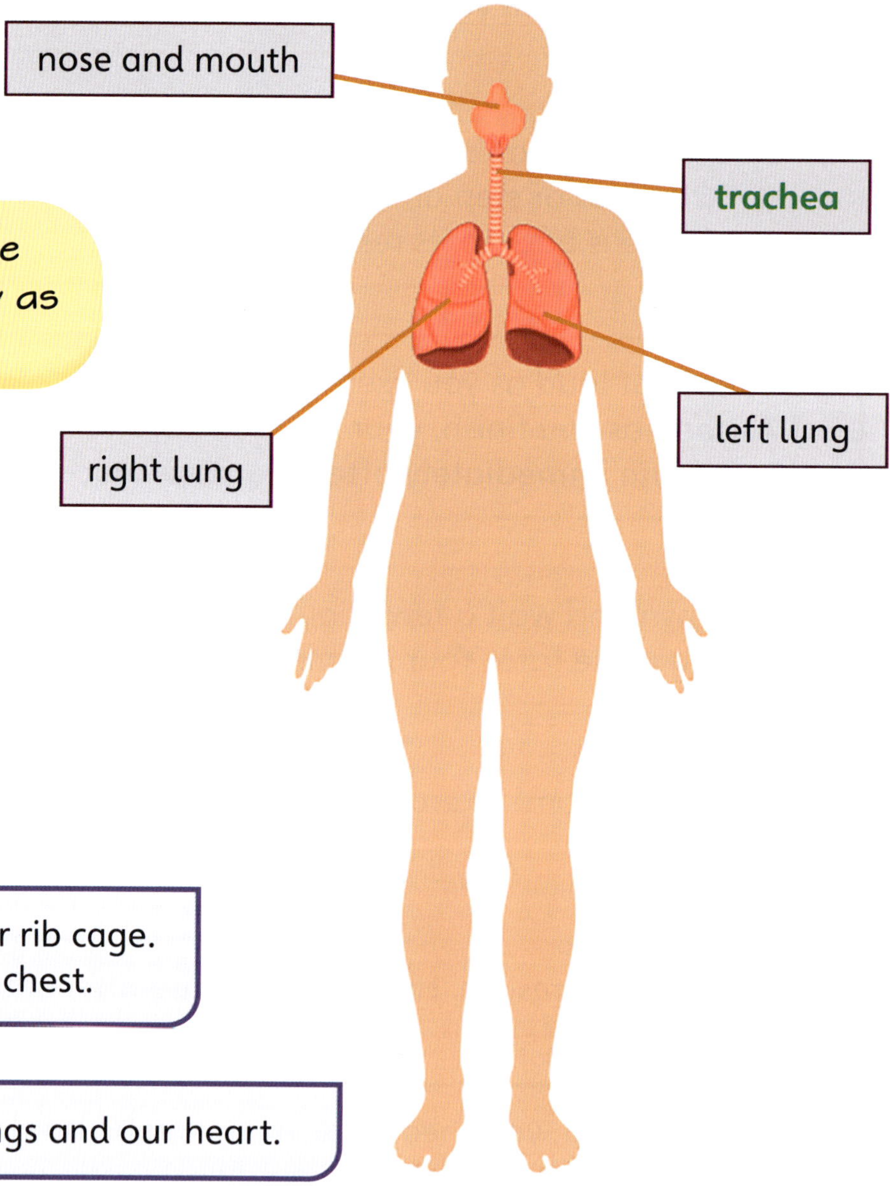

Our thorax is the **space** inside our rib cage. We call this part of the body our chest.

The rib cage protects our two lungs and our heart.

There is a flat, thin muscle across the bottom of our thorax to separate it from our stomach and intestines. This is our **diaphragm**.

Topic 3 | Heart, lungs and circulation

Our lungs are the organs we use for breathing.

Put your hands gently on your chest to feel your rib cage. **Breathe** in. How does your rib cage move?

Now breathe out and feel how it changes.

This diagram shows what happens when you breathe in.

When the rib cage and diaphragm move, it makes more space inside the thorax.

Air is pulled in to fill the extra space.

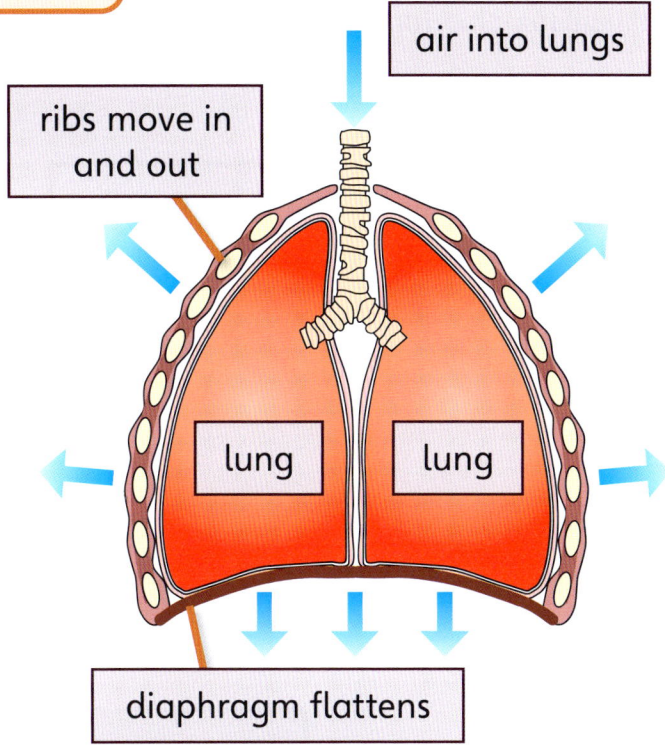

air into lungs

ribs move in and out

lung   lung

diaphragm flattens

To breathe out, the rib cage goes back to where it started, so air is pushed back out.

We use muscles to move the rib cage. They contract to move it up and **outwards** and then relax to let it go back down and **inwards** again.

Key words

thorax   trachea   space   diaphragm   breathe   outwards   inwards

Modelling breathing

Breathing is the word we use for taking air in and out of the lungs.

Sometimes breathing is called ventilating the lungs or **ventilation**.

This is a **model** of our thorax.
It is made with a glass jar and some balloons.

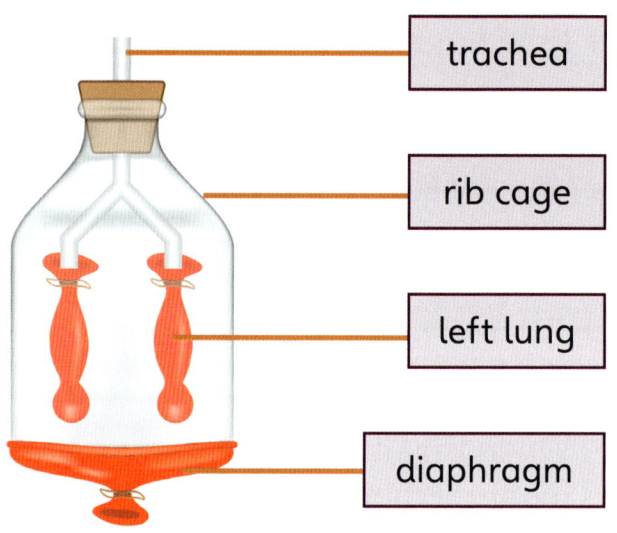

- trachea
- rib cage
- left lung
- diaphragm

When someone pulls the diaphragm down there is more space in the jar for air.

Air enters through the tube at the top (trachea) and **inflates** the balloons (lungs).

When the diaphragm is let go there is not enough space for all the air that came in. Air goes back out of the trachea.

Talk about the model with partner.
Can you see anything wrong with the model?
Can you see something that is not moving?

Topic 3 | Heart, lungs and circulation

You can try making a simpler model like this. It shows one lung instead of two.

You will need:
- a large plastic bottle
- two balloons
- scissors.

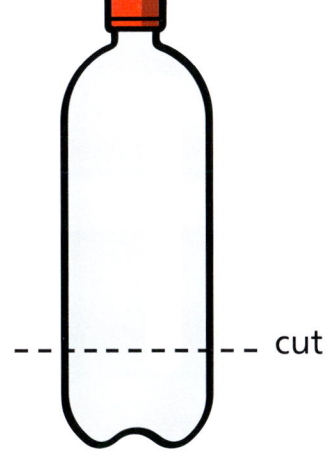
cut

1. Cut the bottom off the bottle.

2. Cut the wider end off one balloon and tie a knot at the other end.

3. Stretch this balloon over the wider end of the bottle.

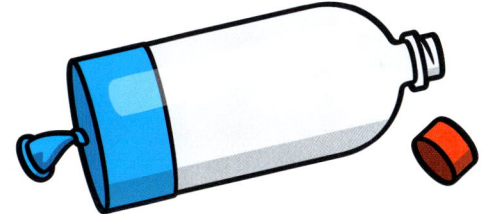

4. Put the other balloon into the top of the bottle with the open end sticking out of the neck of the bottle.

5. Stretch the open end of the balloon over the neck of the bottle.

6. Pull the diaphragm balloon down and watch what happens to the lung balloon.

Key words

ventilation   model   inflates

What happens to the air we breathe in?

Air is a mixture of gases. Oxygen is one of them. We breathe in all the gases of the air, but we only use the oxygen.

The lungs work closely with the circulatory system. In the lungs, oxygen from the air enters the blood.

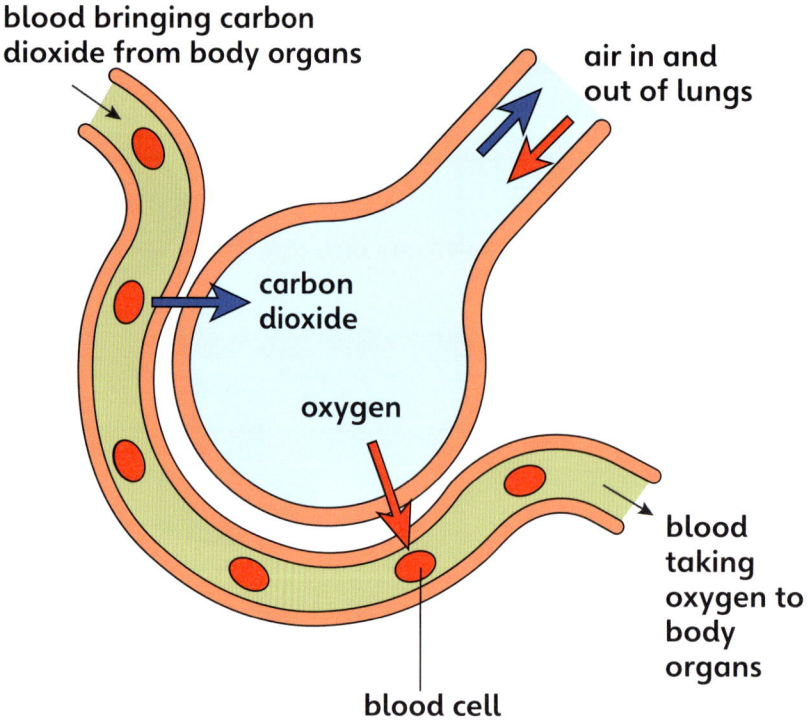

The blood takes the oxygen to body organs such as our brain, stomach or muscles so they can use it. Here it goes, inside this blood vessel.

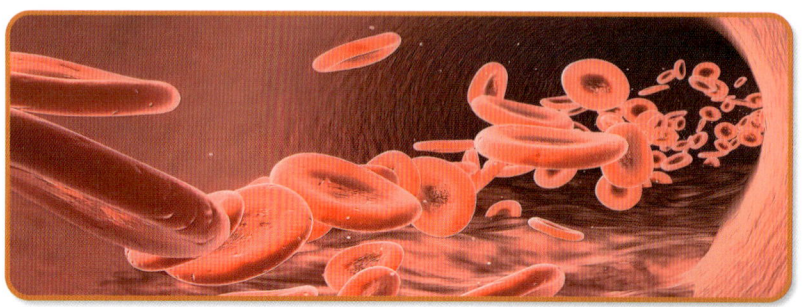

Topic 3 | Heart, lungs and circulation

Here the blood has arrived at a muscle, carrying the oxygen and nutrients. These nutrients were **absorbed** into the blood in the digestive system.

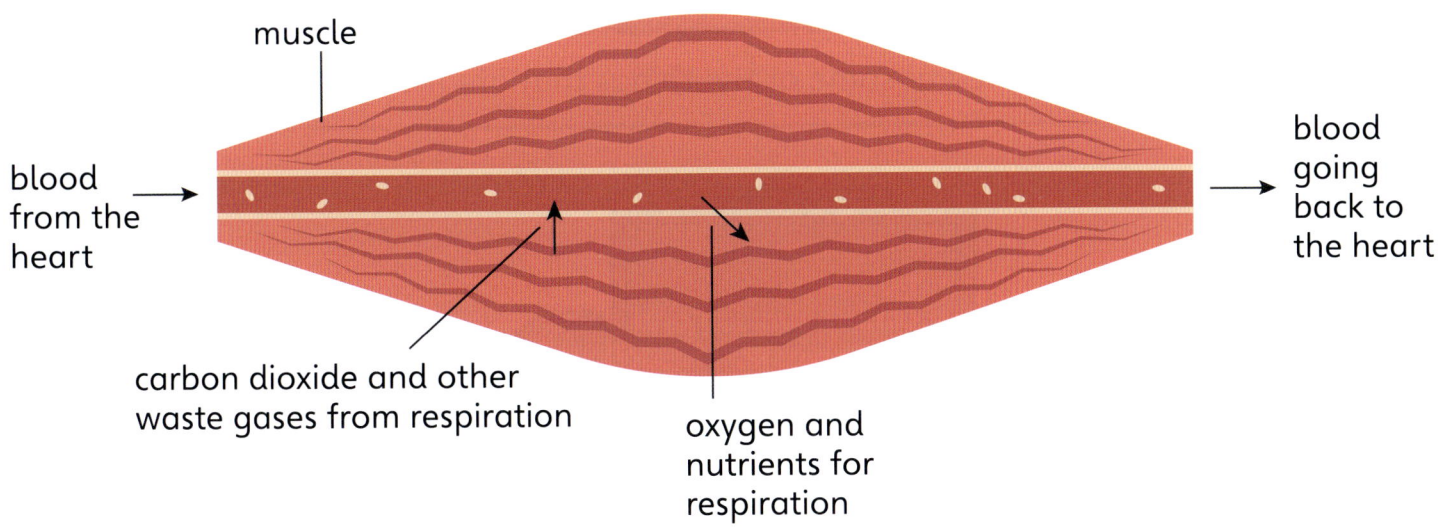

The muscle uses the oxygen, and nutrients like sugars, for the life process of respiration. This gives it the energy to contract.

The muscle puts **waste** from respiration back into the blood.

One of the waste materials is **carbon dioxide** gas. This goes back to the lungs and is breathed out with the rest of the air that we did not use.

Respiration is how the body uses oxygen once it reaches our organs.

Key words

absorbed   waste   carbon dioxide

Transport in our bodies

Transporting means moving things.

In this topic we have looked at some of the things that are moved:

- oxygen
- nutrients
- carbon dioxide and other waste.

And we have looked at the ways they are moved:

- gases are breathed in and out of the lungs

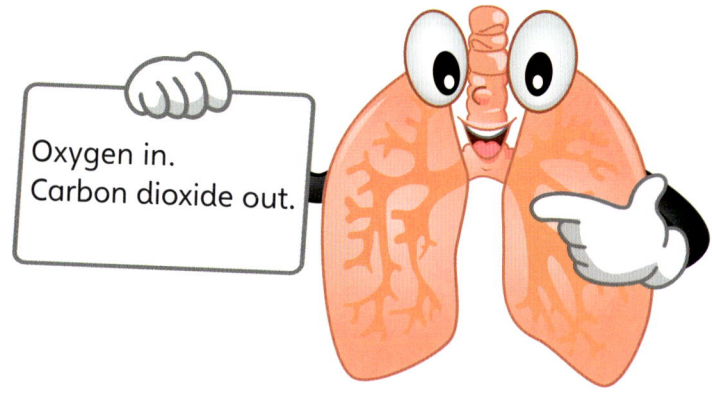

Oxygen in. Carbon dioxide out.

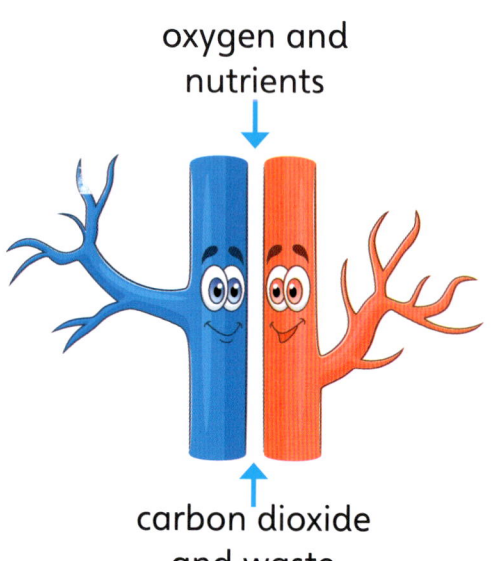

oxygen and nutrients

carbon dioxide and waste

- useful materials and waste are transported around our body by blood in blood vessels.

50

Topic 3 | Heart, lungs and circulation

Now let's look at how the respiratory system and circulatory system work together.

Blood that goes to the lungs and blood that goes to the body organs has to travel along very **narrow** blood vessels.

Imagine your whole school out on the playground having to walk through a narrow tunnel to go back inside. You would all be slowed down a bit!

So blood needs an extra push from the heart to make sure it reaches your feet, and the top of your head and your fingers.

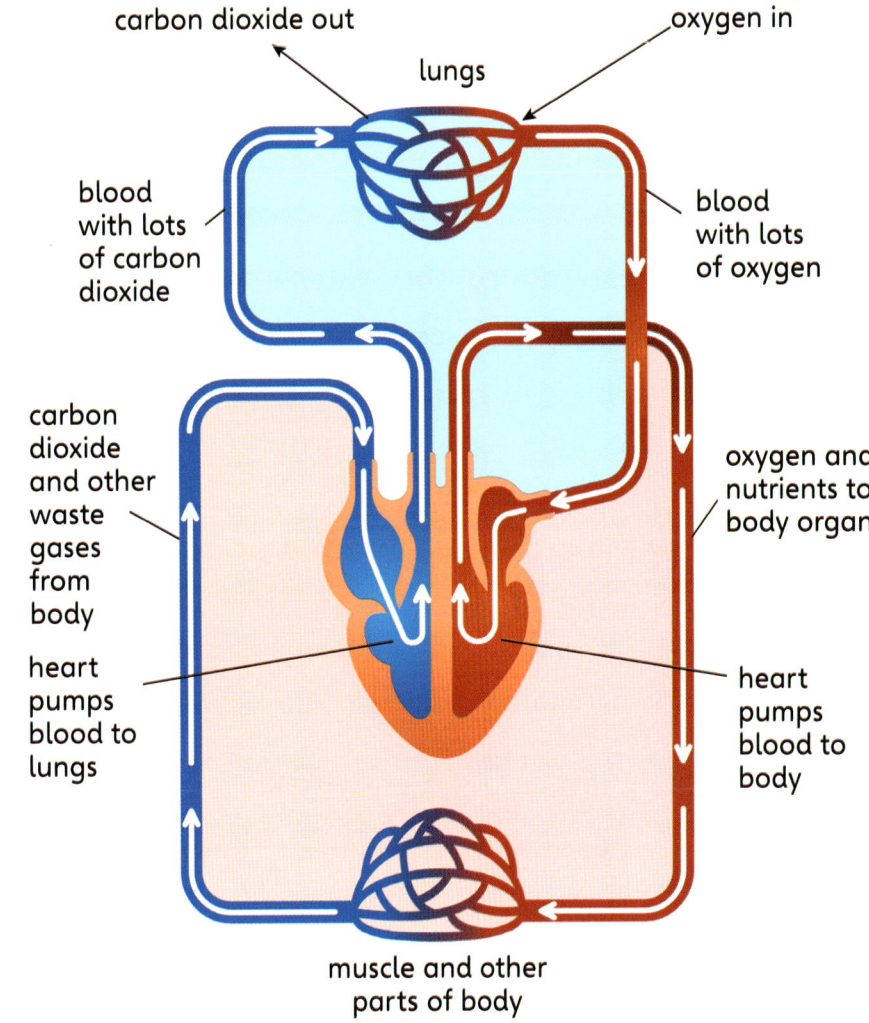

carbon dioxide out
oxygen in
lungs
blood with lots of carbon dioxide
blood with lots of oxygen
carbon dioxide and other waste gases from body
oxygen and nutrients to body organs
heart pumps blood to lungs
heart pumps blood to body
muscle and other parts of body

Feel your heart beating in your chest or listen to a **heartbeat** sound. Can you hear two parts to each heartbeat? Duh-dum, duh-dum, duh-dum …

This shows the heart is doing two pumps of blood at the same time. One to the lungs and one to the body.

Key words

transporting   narrow   heartbeat

51

End of topic questions

Heart, lungs and circulation

Graphs are a good way to show patterns and trends. A trend means *how the results change over time*.

When we do investigations about pulse rate or breathing rate we are interested in how the pattern changes over a period of time.

Look at these graphs with a partner. Take turns to:

- describe what is shown on each graph by looking at the axis labels; use them to think of a title for each graph
- describe how the graph line goes up or down over time
- answer the questions under each graph.

Graph 1

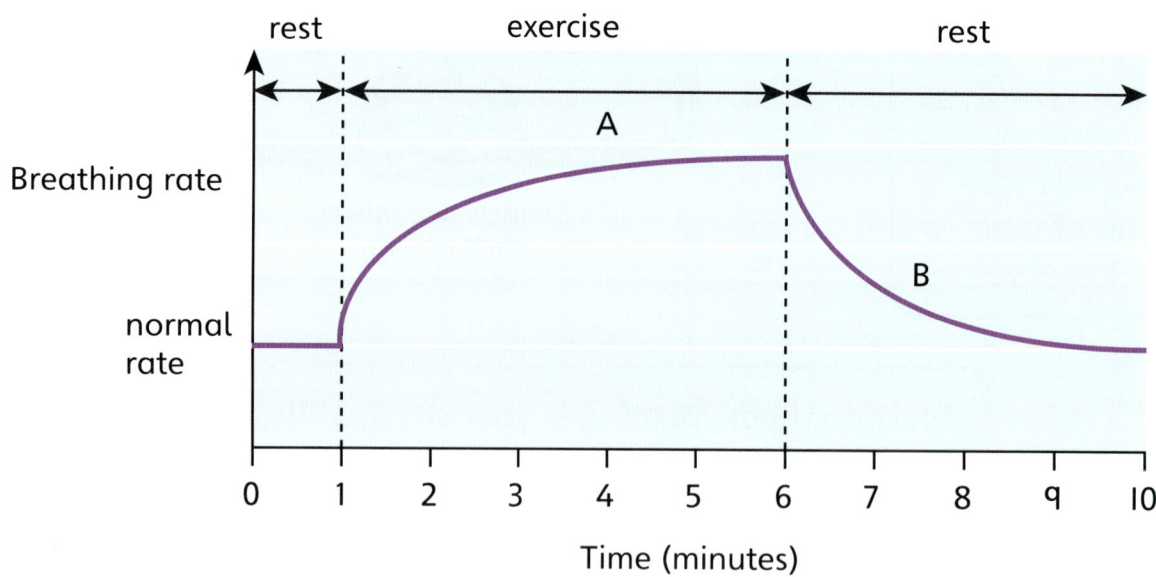

1. How long did this person exercise for?
2. Describe what is happening during parts **A** and **B** and explain why.
3. How long did it take for the person's breathing rate to go back to normal?

Topic 3 | End of topic questions

Graph 2

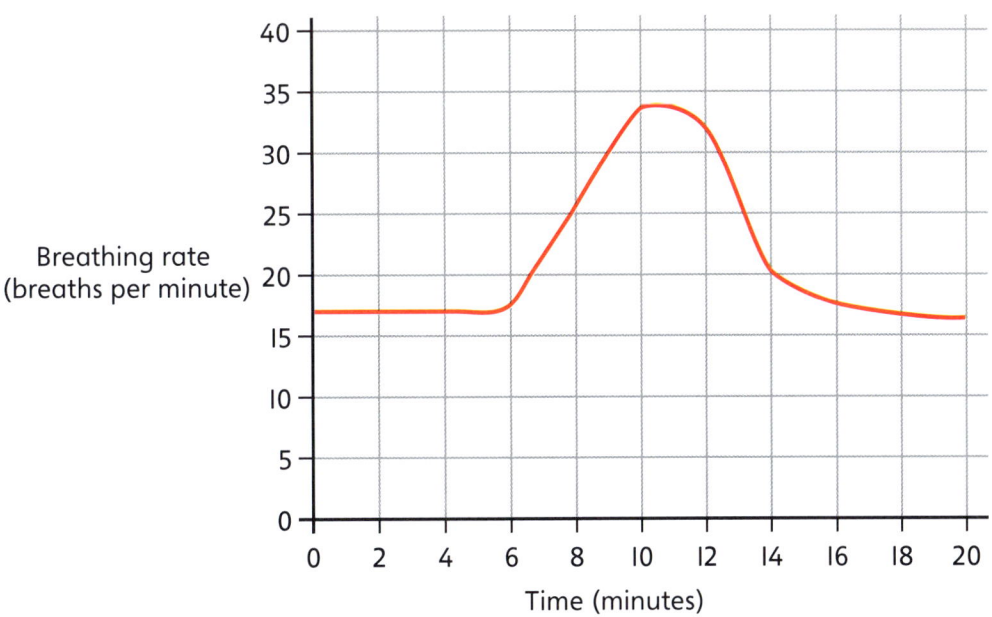

4. What is this person's normal breathing rate?

5. Suggest what happened between 6 and 10 minutes. What evidence do you have to support your suggestion?

Graph 3

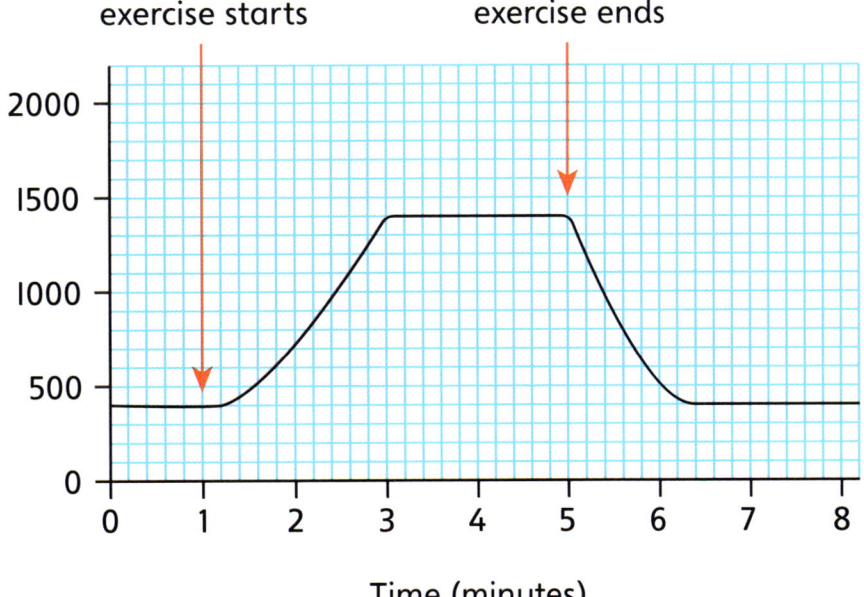

6. What volume of air does this person normally breathe in one minute?

7. How did this change when they exercised? Answer using information from the graph.

4 Reversible and irreversible change

Some changes can be reversed, others cannot. Let's look at some of the ways we can see changes are taking place.

You already know ways of separating mixtures. If you mix sand and water, the sand does not dissolve so you can separate it from the water by filtration. A solution of salt and water can be separated by evaporating the water. Both these changes are reversible. This is like when you make a mistake when typing, and press 'undo' or 'delete' and everything changes back to how it was before.

Not all changes can be reversed. Look at the picture of the bread dough. The dough in the picture is very soft and light. Think about what happens when bread dough is cooked in an oven. It changes colour and changes texture. Now you cannot change it back into dough again.

Think about other things that you see change. When ice melts can it be frozen again? Can eggs go back to what they were like before they were cooked? Do you think that logs burning on a fire can ever change back into logs again?

Sieving or filtration?

Sieving and filtration are two methods of separating materials.

What can you remember about sieving and filtration, Sully?

If two solids have grains of different sizes, use a sieve.

If there is a solid in a liquid but the solid has **not dissolved**, use filtration.

Predict which of these materials can be separated by sieving and which by filtration:
- sand and water
- raisins and flour
- soil and water
- rocks and soil.

Now try separating each mixture in the way you predicted.

Topic 4 | Reversible and irreversible change

Sieving

Choose a sieve with **mesh** that one solid will fit through but the other one will not.

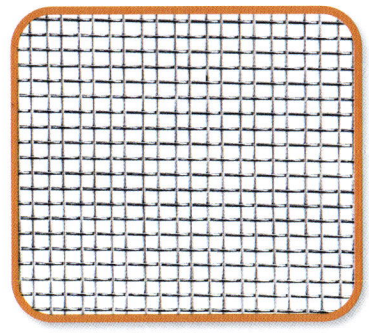

Flour can go through the holes in the sieve.

Seeds do not fit through the holes. Seeds stay in the sieve.

Filtration

For filtration you need a **filter funnel** with folded **filter paper** inside it.

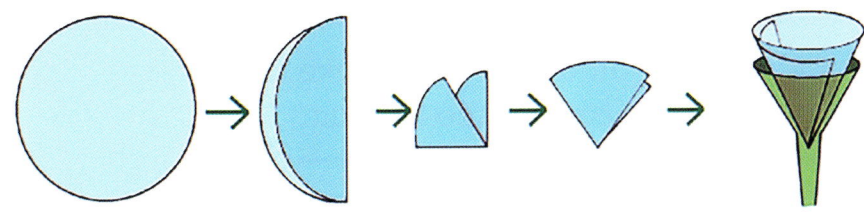

Put this over a container and pour your mixture into the filter funnel.

Water can go through filter paper but a solid that has **not** dissolved cannot.

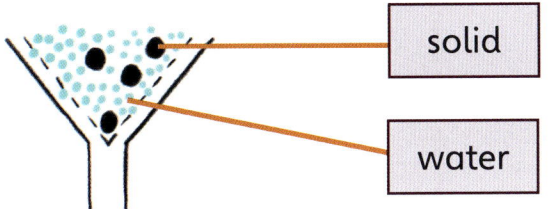

solid

water

filter paper

filter funnel

Key words

sieving | filtration | dissolved | mesh | filter funnel | filter paper

57

Solutions

When we put some solids into a liquid we cannot see them. They make a **solution**.

When we stir sugar into a drink we can no longer see the sugar. The sugar **dissolves**.

When we stir salt into hot water the salt dissolves to make a salt solution. Once that happens we cannot see the salt.

A scientist is using this chemical.

She puts some of the chemical into a beaker of warm water.

Why does she use **warm** water?

Topic 4 | Reversible and irreversible change

She stirs it until all the chemical dissolves. She has made a solution.

We use the word **solute** to describe the solid that dissolves.

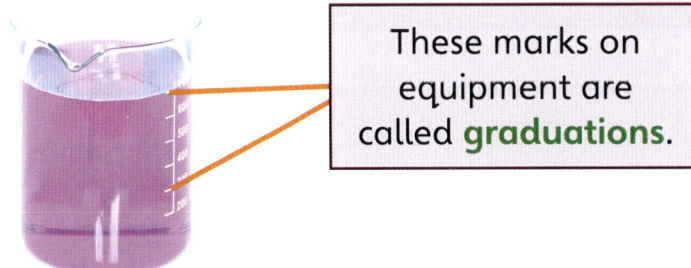

These marks on equipment are called **graduations**.

The liquid it dissolves in is called a **solvent**.

solvent

solute

When a solute dissolves in a solvent it makes a solution.

solution

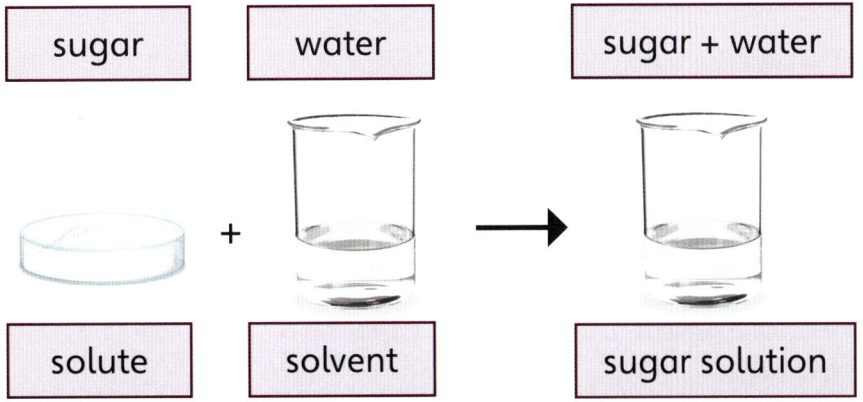

sugar — solute

water — solvent

sugar + water — sugar solution

We only use these words for solids that can dissolve.

A solid that cannot dissolve is **insoluble**. Sand and flour are both insoluble in water.

Key words

solution   dissolves   graduations   solute   solvent   insoluble

Finding the dissolved solute

We can find the dissolved solute in a salt solution.

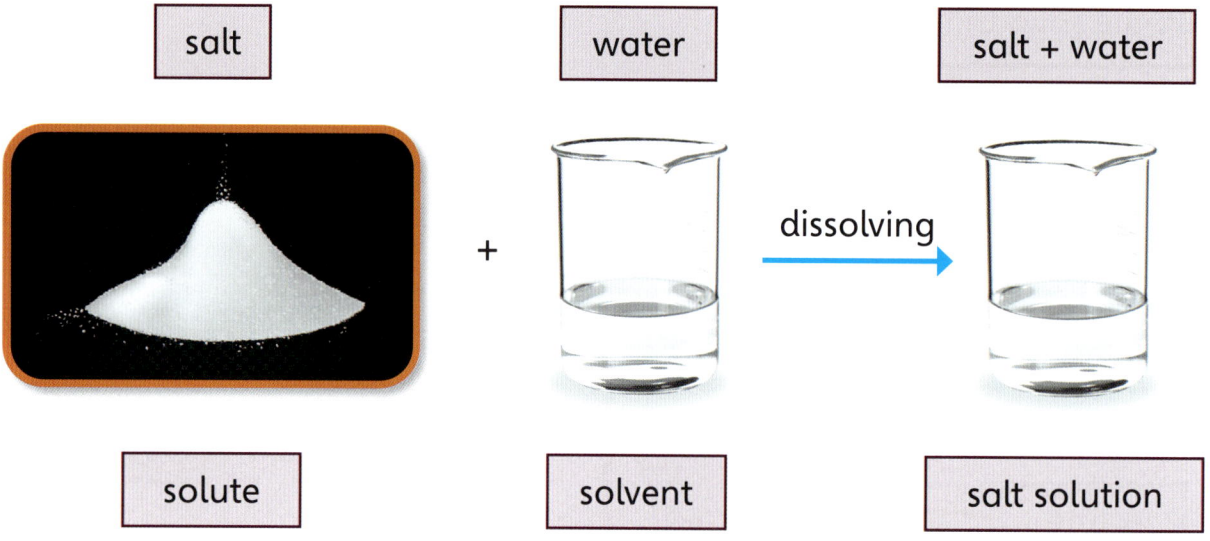

We cannot see the salt when it has dissolved in the water. The salt is **soluble**.

Let's find the dissolved solute.

You will need:
- some **rock salt** (grit salt)
- a rolling pin and a small, strong bag, or a **pestle and mortar**
- two beakers and a spoon or stirrer
- hot water from your teacher
- a filter funnel and filter paper
- an **evaporating dish**
- a **hand lens**.

Rock salt is a mixture of salt and bits of sand or rock.

Topic 4 | Reversible and irreversible change

1. Crush the rock salt into small pieces in the bag using the rolling pin, or use a pestle and mortar.

2. Put the rock salt into a beaker of hot water. Stir.

What will dissolve?
What will not dissolve?

3. Pour the contents of your beaker into a filter funnel over beaker 2.

What stays in the filter paper?
What goes through?

4. Pour the clear liquid from beaker 2 into the evaporating dish. This is your salt solution.

5. Leave the evaporating dish in a warm place. Check it regularly to see when all the water has evaporated.

6. Look at your salt crystals using a hand lens.

Key words

soluble   rock salt   pestle and mortar   evaporating dish   hand lens

States of matter

All the materials and all the other things in the world such as air and water are called **matter**.

You already found out about the three different states of matter: **solid**, **liquid**, **gas**.

Solids

Solids have a fixed shape. They keep their shape in different containers.

We cannot **pour** solids.

Solids cannot be **compressed**.

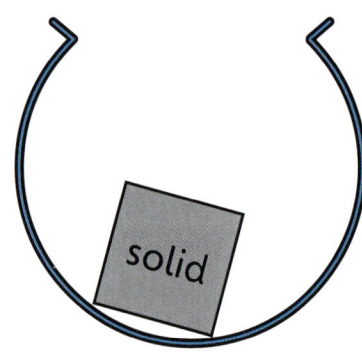

Liquids

Liquids can be poured. They can change their shape. Liquids take the shape of their container.

Liquids can **flow**. They make a **pool** when they are not in a container.

Liquids cannot be compressed easily.

Topic 4 | Reversible and irreversible change

Gases

Gases can change shape. A gas can be poured. Gases move around and fill the space they are in.

A gas can be compressed.

lid

brown gas

Changing state

Matter can **change state**. A change of temperature is needed to do this.

Scientists describe changes of state as **reversible changes**. They are changes that can be changed back or **undone**.

Undo means you can change back to what was there before.

Dissolving and mixing are also reversible changes. We will look at these later in the topic.

Key words

matter   solid   liquid   gas   pour   compressed

flow   pool   change state   reversible changes   undone

Changes of state

Melting and freezing are reversible changes.

The change of state from solid to liquid is called melting.

The opposite change of state, from liquid to solid, is called freezing.

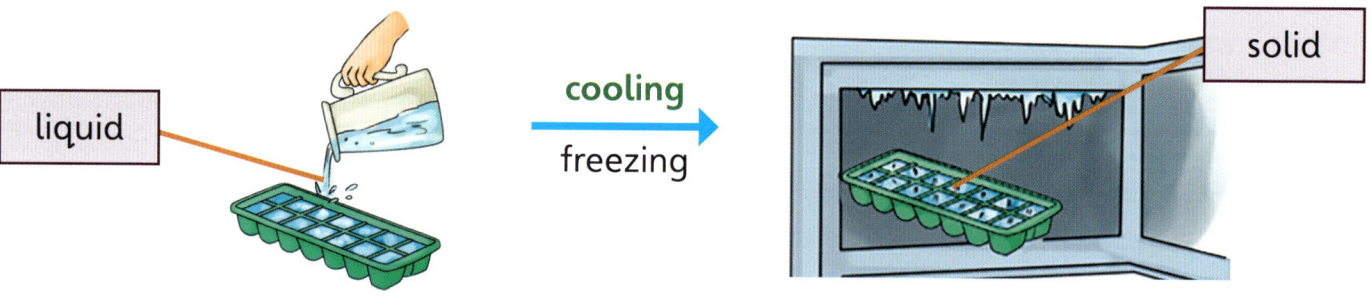

Evaporation and condensation are reversible changes.

The change of state from a liquid to a gas is called evaporation.

bubbles of gas in boiling water

Topic 4 | Reversible and irreversible change

The opposite change of state, from gas to liquid, is called condensation. Water vapour is invisible. We see evidence of it when it condenses on the cold lid. It also condenses in the cooler air above the pan and on cold objects such as this window.

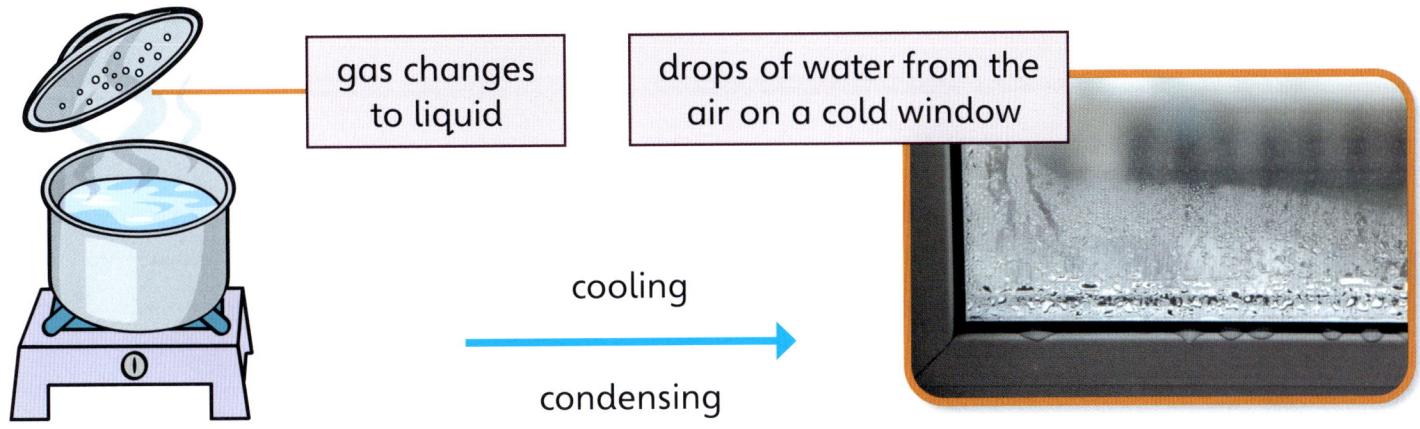

gas changes to liquid

drops of water from the air on a cold window

cooling / condensing

This diagram summarises all these reversible changes for water.

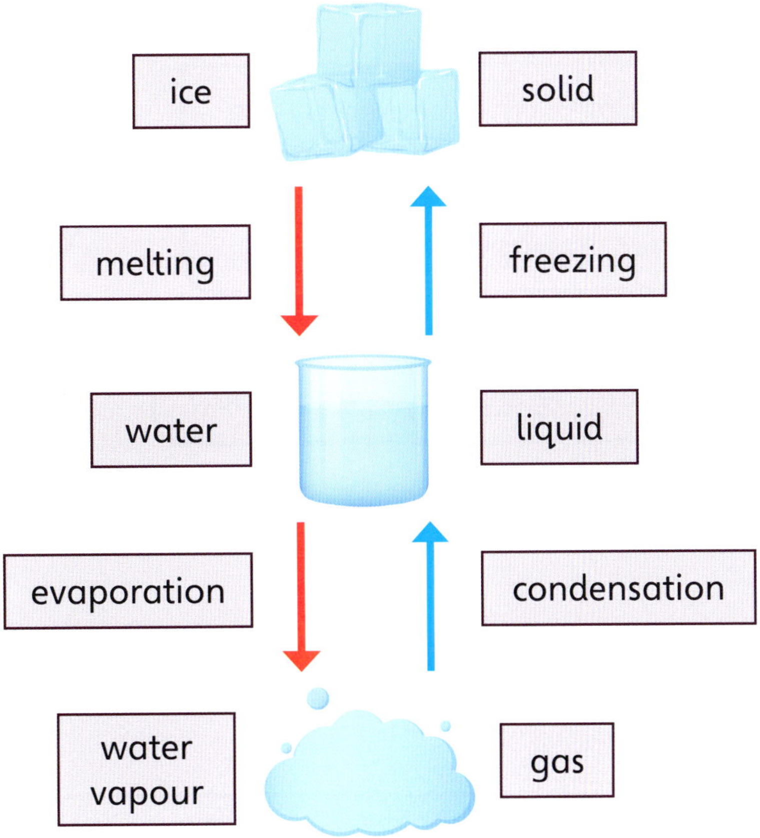

- ice — solid
- melting / freezing
- water — liquid
- evaporation / condensation
- water vapour — gas

Which arrows show heating?

Which arrows show cooling?

Key words

melting | freezing | heating | cooling | evaporation | condensation

65

The water cycle

The **water cycle** is the path that all the water on Earth follows as it changes from one state to another.

We have met the idea of a cycle before.

Animals and plants have life cycles. Decomposers recycle useful materials.

Water on the surface of Earth is heated by the Sun. This causes the liquid water in streams, rivers, seas and oceans to change state to become water vapour. It evaporates.

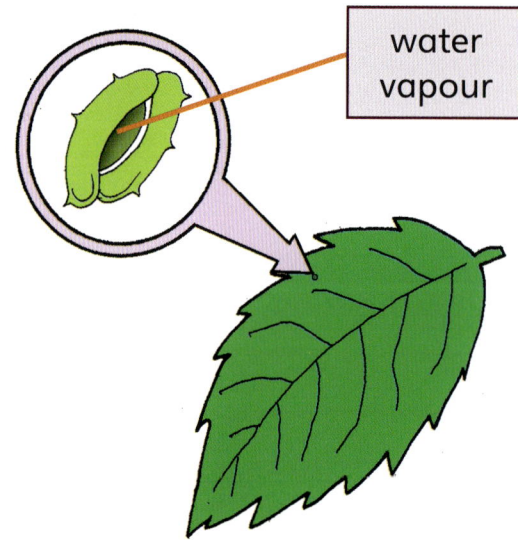

water vapour

Water evaporates from the leaves of plants too.

Think how many leaves there are on just one tree.

All this water vapour goes up higher and higher into the **atmosphere**. The atmosphere is the layers of air above the Earth.

Topic 4 | Reversible and irreversible change

High above Earth, the atmosphere is much cooler.
The water vapour condenses from a gas to a liquid, forming **clouds**.

Water from these clouds falls to Earth as **rain**.
If the water cools much more in the clouds it falls as a solid – we see **hail** or **snow**.
Rain, hail and snow are different types of **precipitation**.

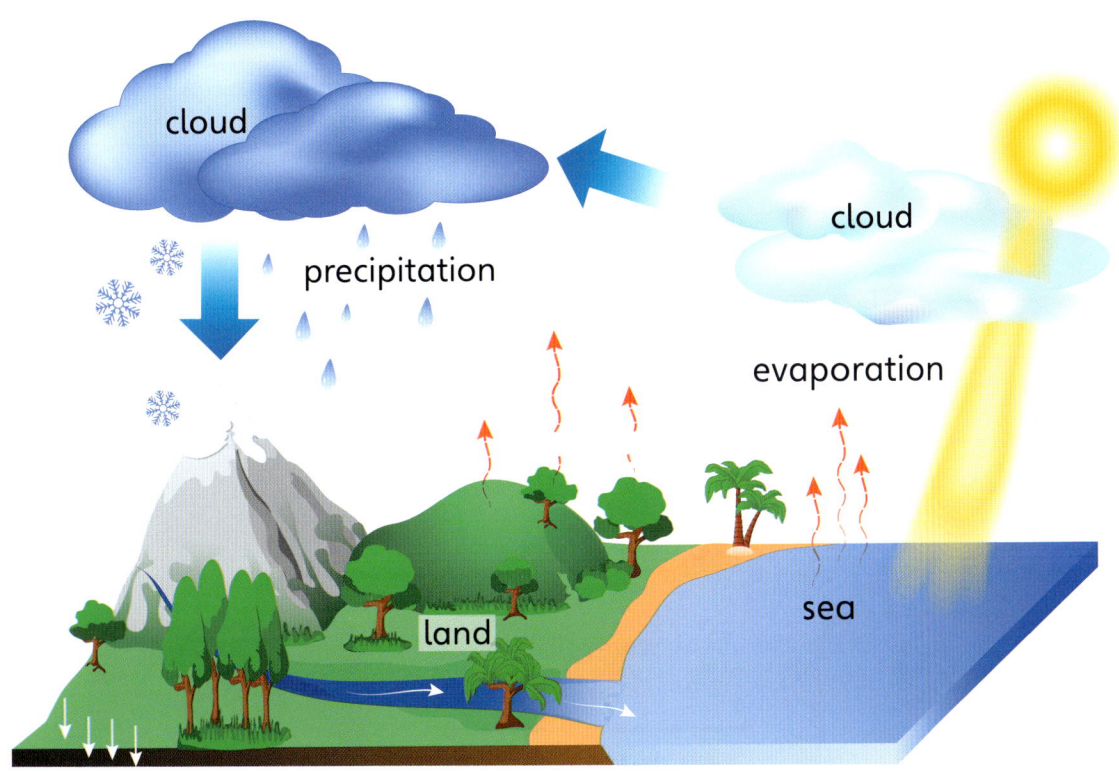

The rain puts water back into the streams, rivers, seas and oceans.
It also puts water back into the soil for plant roots to take up again.

Key words

water cycle   atmosphere   clouds   rain   hail   snow   precipitation

Irreversible changes

Some changes in materials are **irreversible**.

This kind of change usually cannot be reversed.
The materials cannot go back to how they were before the change.

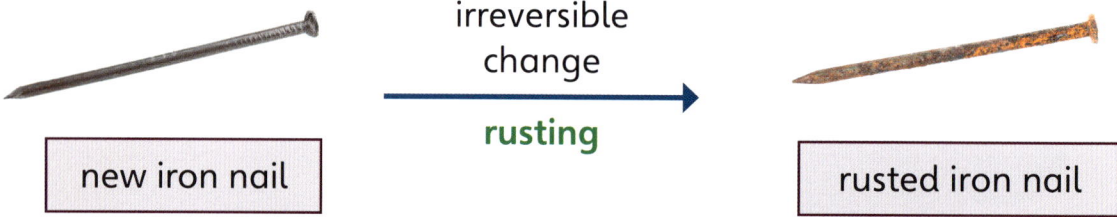

new iron nail — irreversible change **rusting** → rusted iron nail

The rusty iron nail cannot go back to being a new iron nail because a **new material**, rust, has been made.

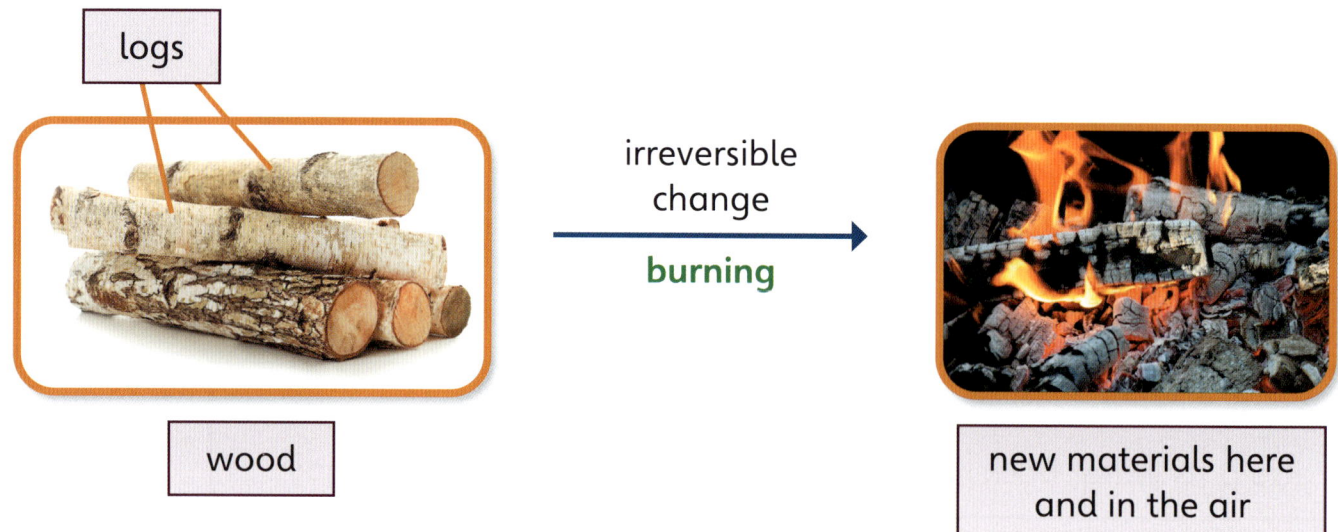

logs / wood — irreversible change **burning** → new materials here and in the air

The burnt wood cannot go back to being a log again.
Burning the logs makes new materials.

Topic 4 | Reversible and irreversible change

Bread dough changes when it is cooked.

dough

irreversible change
cooking

bread

The bread is a new material.
It cannot go back to being dough again.

Irreversible changes are **chemical changes**.

One way to know whether a chemical change has happened is to look for new materials being made.

cement mix

water added

irreversible change

chemical change

hard cement floor

The cement and water change to make the new hard material. The change produces heat. This heat is evidence that an irreversible chemical change has taken place.

Key words

irreversible   rusting   new material   burning   cooking   chemical changes

69

Investigating irreversible changes

Irreversible changes can be called **chemical reactions**.

You have already seen the reaction between cement and water. A temperature change takes place and a new, hard material is formed.

Sometimes we see evidence of an irreversible change when the new material is a different colour from the materials we started with.

Iron is a hard grey metal.

Rust is orange and brown. Bits break off easily.

The colour and the texture have changed irreversibly.

Topic 4 | Reversible and irreversible change

Some irreversible changes produce more than one new material.

One of the new materials may be a gas.
Bubbles of gas are evidence of a new material being formed.

- white vinegar
- bubbles of carbon dioxide gas
- bicarbonate of soda

1. Put 8 tablespoons of white **vinegar** (an acid) into a small glass beaker.

2. Put a thermometer into the liquid and measure the temperature.

3. Add 2 teaspoons of **bicarbonate of soda**. Does the temperature change?

What are the two pieces of evidence you have that an irreversible chemical change is taking place?

Key words

chemical reactions   vinegar   bicarbonate of soda

71

More carbon dioxide

Here are two investigations for you to try using white vinegar and bicarbonate of soda to make carbon dioxide gas.

For both investigations, you will need:

- measuring spoons
- bicarbonate of soda
- a small funnel
- a balloon
- white vinegar
- a small plastic bottle
- red food colouring
- a measuring cylinder
- a party hat or other cone shaped object, or modelling clay
- a tray or wide sink for working in (or work outside).

Use carbon dioxide to inflate a balloon

1. Put 2 tablespoons of bicarbonate of soda into the balloon, using the funnel.

2. Clean the funnel, then use it to put vinegar into the bottle. Make it about 4 cm deep, but not more than one-third full.

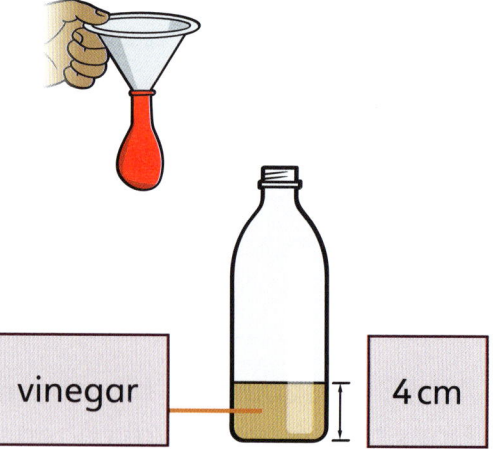

3. Stretch the neck of the balloon over the bottle without letting the contents fall out.

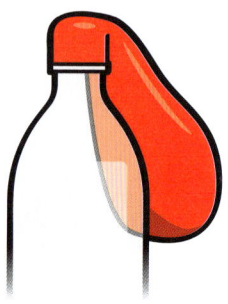

Topic 4 | Reversible and irreversible change

4. Hold the balloon up and let the contents fall into the bottle.

5. If you repeat the investigation, wash out the bottle and start with new vinegar and bicarbonate of soda each time.

Make a volcano

1. Use the funnel to put 2 tablespoons of bicarbonate of soda into the bottle.

2. Cut the top off a cone-shaped party hat so it fits over the bottle. You could make the cone out of card instead or use modelling clay to make your volcano.

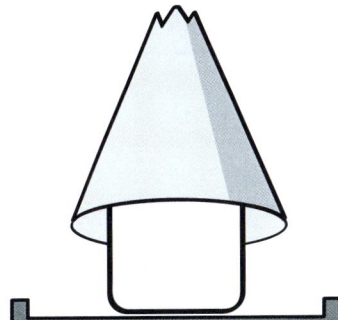

3. Put 2 or 3 drops of food colouring into 60 cm³ vinegar.

4. Pour the coloured vinegar into the bottle in the centre of your volcano and watch it erupt.

Try changing how much vinegar or bicarbonate of soda you use.
Observe any difference this makes. Remember to change one at a time, not both.

Comparing reversible and irreversible changes

Reversible changes are physical changes. No new materials are formed.
Irreversible changes are chemical changes. One or more new materials are formed.

A reversible change is one that can be changed back to how it was before. Examples of reversible changes we have seen are:
- melting and freezing
- evaporation and condensation.

Other examples of reversible changes are:
- mixing
- dissolving.

Mixing

The change is **reversed** by filtration.

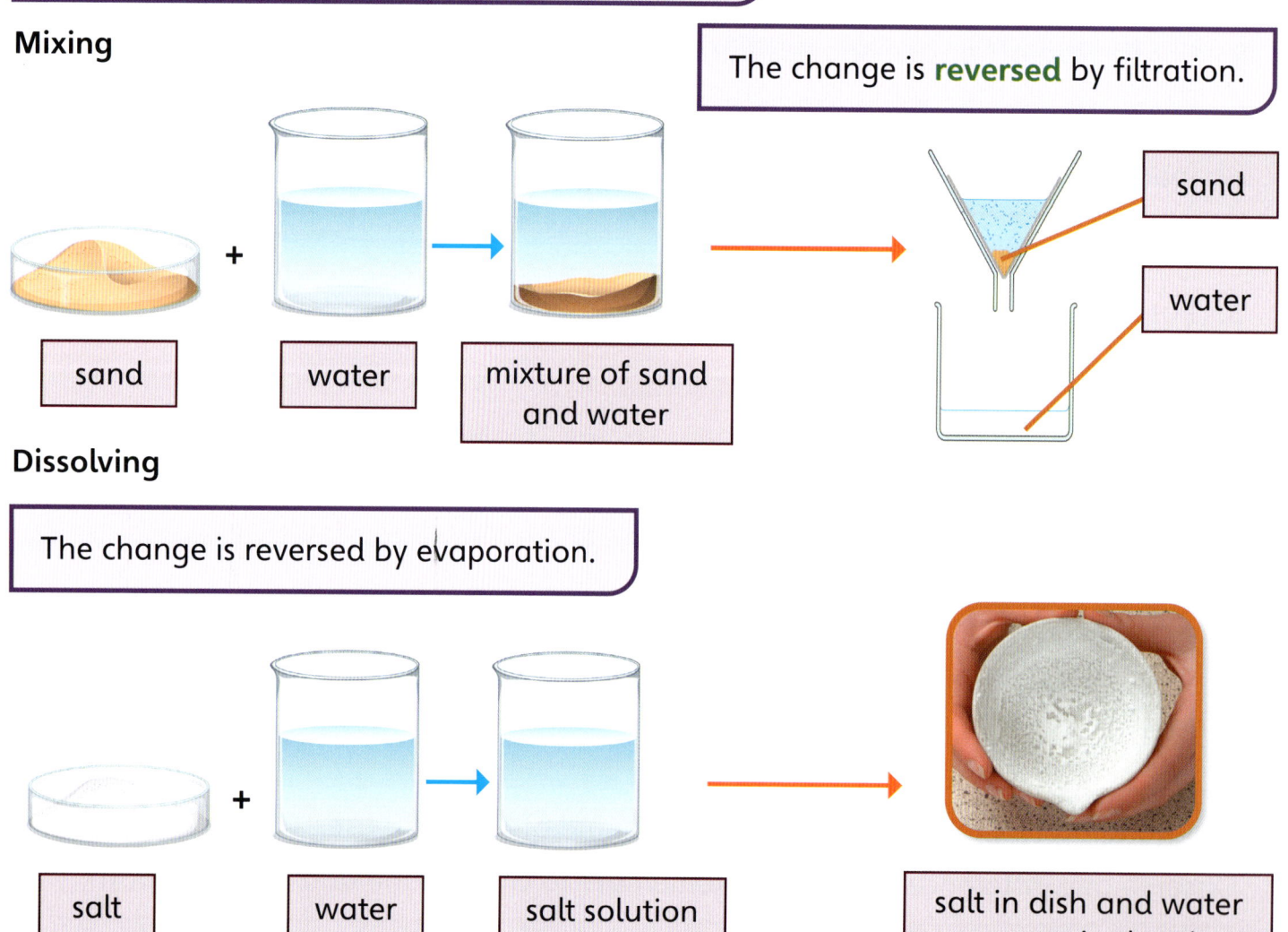

sand + water → mixture of sand and water → sand / water

Dissolving

The change is reversed by evaporation.

salt + water → salt solution → salt in dish and water vapour in the air

74

Topic 4 | Reversible and irreversible change

We can see evidence of irreversible changes by looking for:
- a temperature change
- a colour change
- bubbles of a gas.

liquid wax

solid wax

Candles show both sorts of change. Candles are made of a solid called **wax**.

When the candle is lit, some of the solid wax melts. It changes to a liquid that flows down the sides of the candle. The liquid wax cools and becomes a solid again. Melting wax is a **reversible change**.

Candles do not last forever because some of the wax burns. New materials are formed that go into the air. Burning wax is an **irreversible** change.

The arrows show new materials going into the air. The candle becomes smaller and smaller as the new materials go into the air.

Key words

reversed   wax

End of topic questions

Reversible and irreversible change

1 Work through this section with a partner.

We know that salt and sugar are soluble solids. This means that they dissolve in water.

- Can you remember three ways of making a solute dissolve faster?
- How can you get the salt or sugar back from the solution?

We know that sand and flour are insoluble solids. This means that they do not dissolve in water.

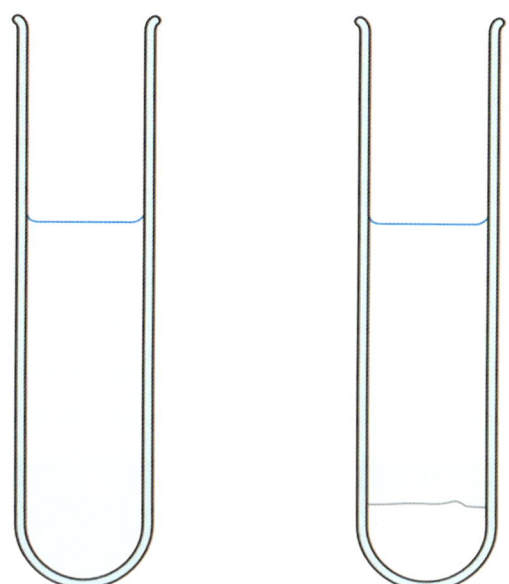

Look at test tubes **A** and **B**. They both contain a solid and some water.

- In which test tube has all the solid dissolved? How did you decide?

A learner is finding out more about dissolving.

This is the scientific question she is investigating.

How many grams of solid dissolve in water at different temperatures?

- What should she change in her investigation?
- What should she measure?
- How will she know if all the solid has dissolved?
- What should she keep the same to make it a fair comparison?
- Why should she repeat her investigation?

When she has completed the investigation she plots this graph.

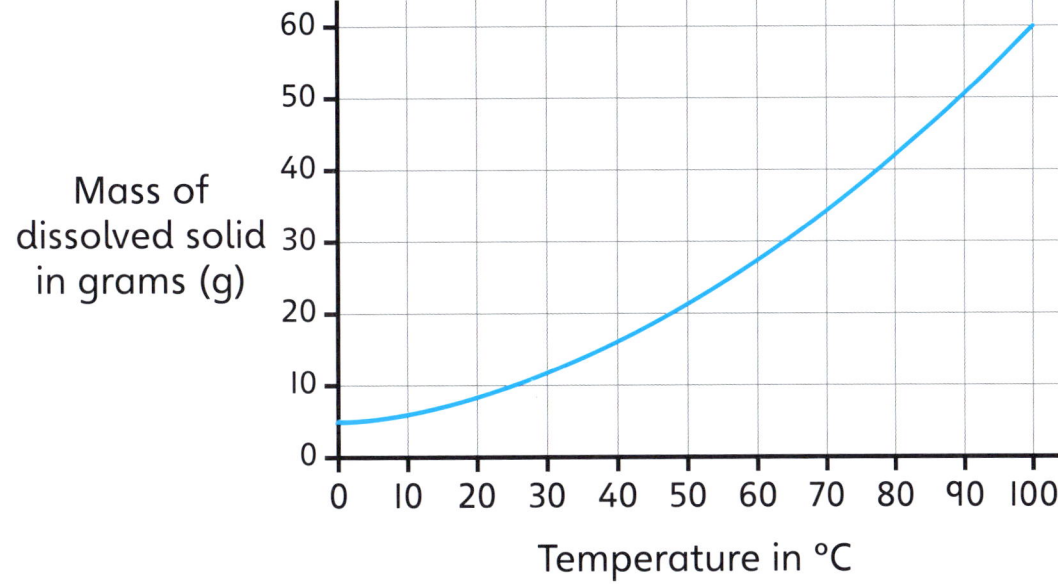

- Suggest a title for the graph.
- Describe the pattern of the results using the words **higher** and **more** in your description.
- How much of this solid dissolved at 70 °C?
- At what temperature did 10 g of this solid dissolve?

5 Forces in air and water

Forces are needed to make objects move. Let's look at more of them.

Have you ever thought about how when you drop something it always falls downwards? This is because the force of gravity pulls falling objects towards the centre of the Earth.

Friction is an invisible contact force that slows moving objects. Objects moving through air or through water are slowed by forces too.

Look at the picture showing a muddy field. What do you think has made the lines in the mud? What were its tyres like? Do you have any shoes or boots with patterns like this on them? Do you wear them in places that are slippery or muddy?

Forces acting on an object

Pushes and pulls are **forces**. The bigger the push or pull, the bigger the force.

When you push an object it moves away from you.

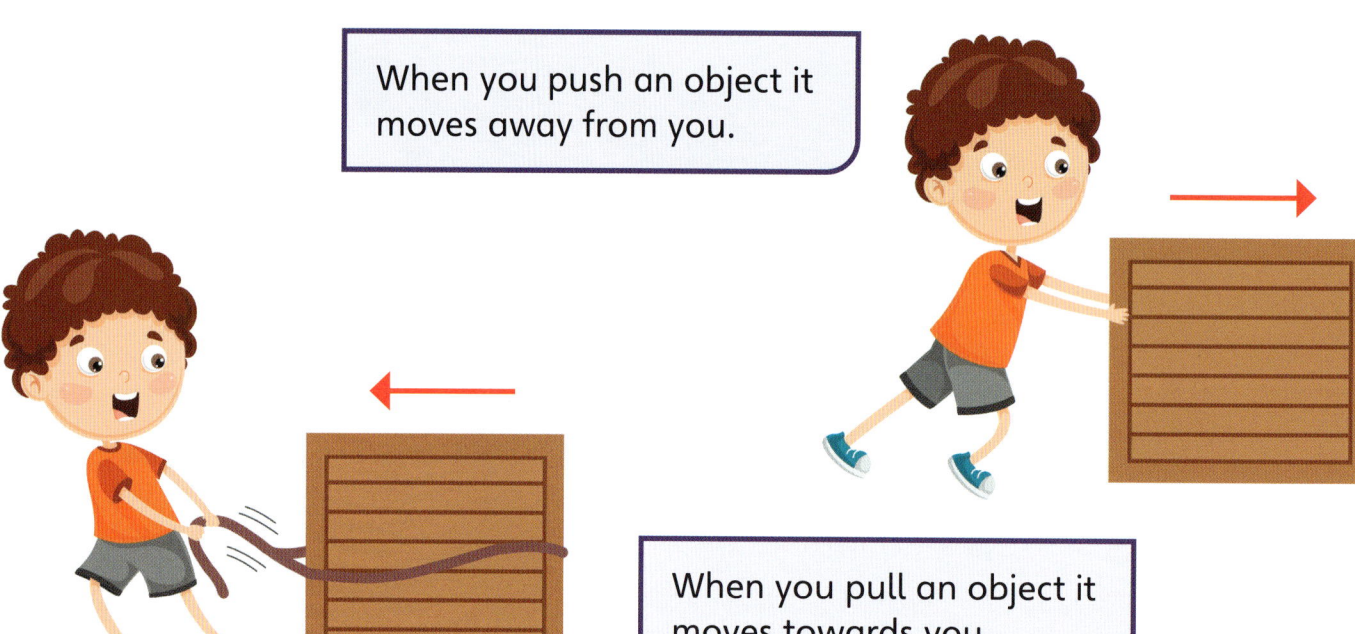

When you pull an object it moves towards you.

Are forces just big or small?

No, forces have a direction too.

When we show a force **acting** on an object we draw an arrow.
The direction of the arrow shows the direction in which the force is acting.
The longer the arrow, the **stronger** the force.

Topic 5 | Forces in air and water

More than one force can act on an object at the same time.

This box has two equal forces acting on it.

In which direction do they act?

The forces on the box are the same **strength** and act in opposite directions. The box does not move because the forces on it are **balanced**.

If one person pushes harder, the forces are no longer balanced and the box moves.

The arrows show that these children are both pushing with the same force.

They do not move apart. The pushing forces are balanced.

Key words

forces   direction   acting   stronger   strength   balanced

Gravity

Have you noticed that when an object falls it goes down to the ground?

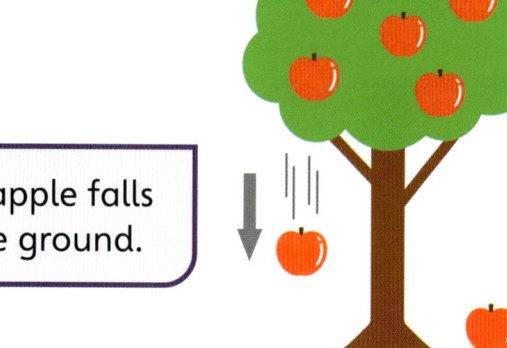

This apple falls to the ground.

But the apple on the ground never moves up to the tree!

Let's think about this on a bigger scale. Imagine you have an apple tree to look at.

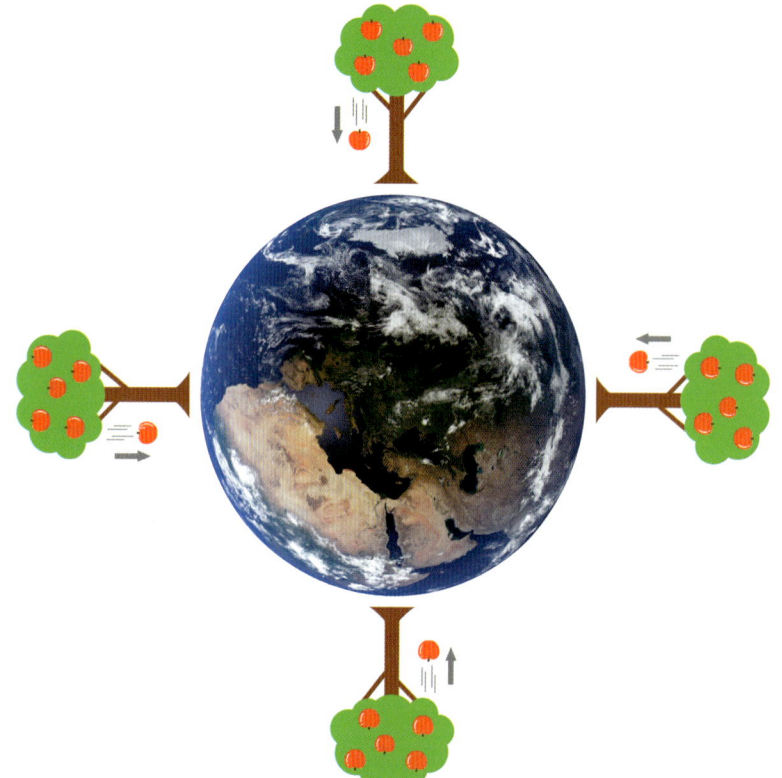

Wherever you are on Earth, your apples fall to the ground.

Apples from your tree fall towards the Earth.

When they reach the ground they cannot move down any further.

Topic 5 | Forces in air and water

Gravity is the invisible force that pulls everything down towards the centre of the Earth.

Like magnetism, gravity is a non-contact force.
Gravity acts between the Earth and the falling object, but they do not need to touch.

If you jump up in the air, this gravitational force pulls you back down.

Think about what would happen if there was no gravitational force to pull you back down.

The force of gravity is weaker on the Moon than on Earth.

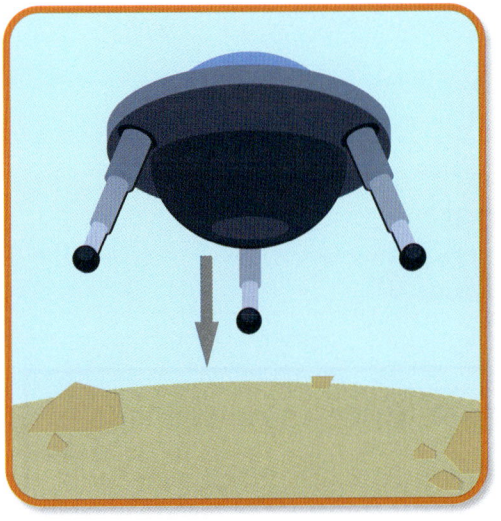

Other planets have gravitational forces of different strengths.

That's how I land. I switch the engines off and down I come.

Gravitational forces keep all the planets in orbit around the Sun, and the Moon in orbit around Earth.

Key words

gravity   invisible   non-contact   gravitational   weaker   strengths

83

Weight

All objects are made of matter. The amount of matter in an object is called its **mass**. The more matter in an object, the greater its mass.

You are made of the same amount of matter whether you stay on Earth or go to the Moon.

We measure mass in **grams** (g) and **kilograms** (kg).

Weight is a force. It is the force with which gravity acts on an object.

On the Moon, your weight is less than on Earth because the strength of the gravitational force there is lower.

In space, I weigh nothing at all, but I am still there. I still have mass.

We measure forces in **newtons** (N).
We write the unit like this:

newton — lower case
N — upper case

Topic 5 | Forces in air and water

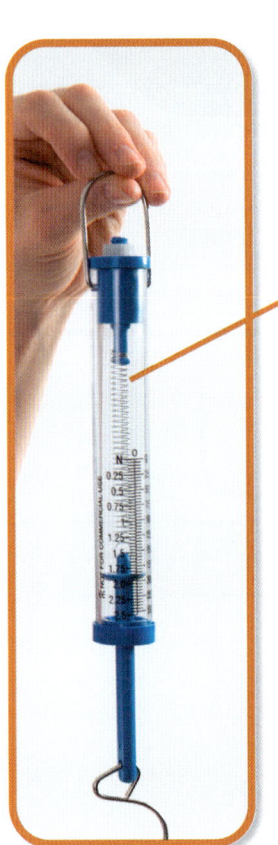

This equipment is called a **force meter** or **newton meter**.

It has a spring inside it.

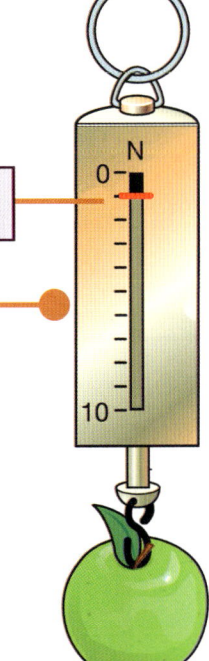

1 newton

This shows a simple diagram of the **scale**.

Look at how to read the scale. When you hang an object on the hook, gravity pulls it downwards.

A force meter is used to measure different forces, not just weight.

This force meter measures the pulling force needed to move the wood along the table.

Use a **force meter** to measure the **weight** in newtons of six different objects.

Now use some **scales** to find out the **mass** of these objects in grams.

Can you see a pattern?

Key words

mass   grams   kilograms (kg)   weight   newtons (N)

force meter   newton meter   scale

85

Friction

Friction is an invisible contact force that acts on objects to slow them down.

You may have investigated the effect of friction by pushing a toy car on different surfaces.

higher friction

lower friction

car moving on **rough** carpet has more friction

same car moving on **smooth** wood has less friction

Try pushing a small object across a surface.

How hard did you have to push to start the object moving?

The force you needed to apply had to be greater than the frictional force stopping the object from moving.

The forces acting on this box are balanced. The box will start to move when the pushing force is stronger than the friction force.

pushing force

friction force

86

Topic 5 | Forces in air and water

Friction can act between other states of matter too, not just solids.

Air resistance causes friction between a solid surface and the air it is moving through.

This aeroplane has a forwards force from its engines acting on it. The force of air resistance acts in the opposite direction.

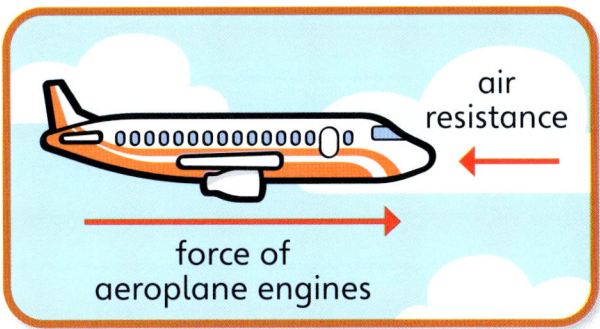

Water resistance causes friction between a solid surface and the water it is moving through.

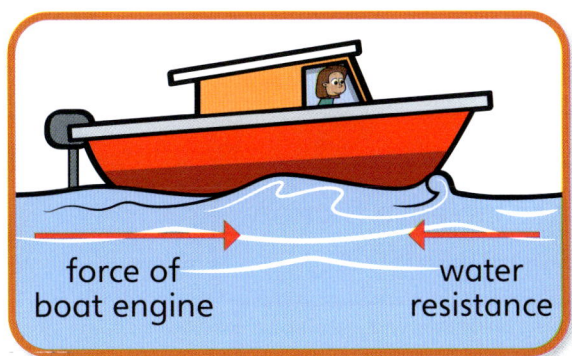

The water resistance force acts on the boat in the opposite direction to the force from its engine.

Key words

friction   rough   smooth   air resistance   water resistance

Investigating grip

Friction slows movement but we sometimes find this useful.

When you write with a pencil there is friction between the graphite and the paper as you try to move the pencil across the page. This causes some of the graphite to stay on the paper as the pencil **grips** the page.

To rub out a mistake, you use friction between the eraser and the paper to take the graphite away.

An HB pencil does not leave much graphite on the paper. 2B to 6B pencils leave more and more graphite, so they draw darker lines.

We use this idea of grip on vehicle tyres.

Tyres with a rougher surface increase friction between the tyre and a slippery surface.

Snow chains give even more grip.

Topic 5 | Forces in air and water

Investigate the grip on some shoes

Shoes are made for different purposes. The bottom of a shoe gives different amounts of grip for different activities or surfaces.

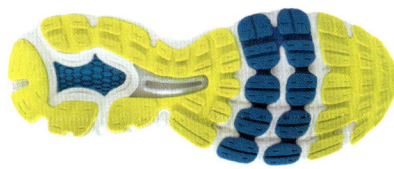

sole

You will need:
- shoes with different **soles**
- a flat surface
- a force meter.

1. Attach the hook of the force meter to the first shoe.

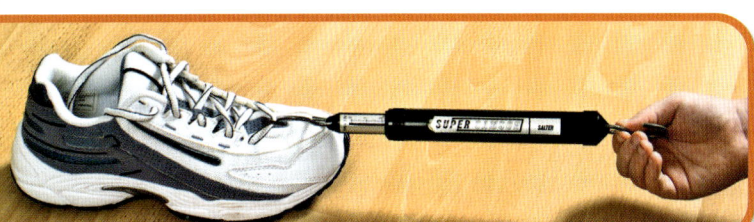

2. Make a start line on your surface.

3. Put the front of the shoe just behind the start line. Check the force meter is in line with the shoe.

4. Measure the force needed to *just* pull the shoe over the line. Repeat this two more times with the same shoe.

5. Repeat steps 3 and 4 for the other shoes. What will you keep the same each time? Think of as many things as you can.

6. Work out the **average** force needed to move each shoe. Can you see a **pattern** between the force needed and the type of sole on the shoe? How could you improve your investigation?

Key words

grips   soles   average   pattern

89

Reducing frictional forces

Air resistance and water resistance are sometimes called **drag** forces. Drag **reduces** the speed at which objects move.

In a **parachute** jump, the size of the air resistance force **increases** when the parachute opens. This slows the speed of the fall.

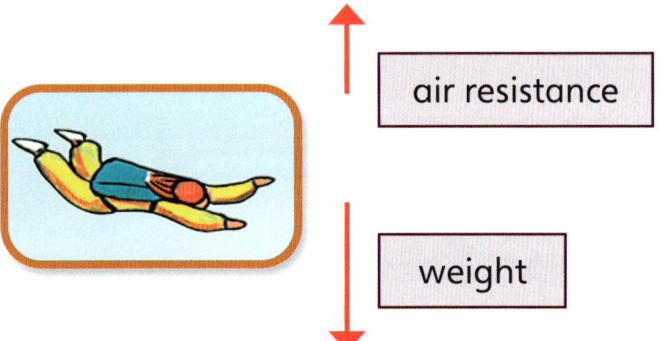

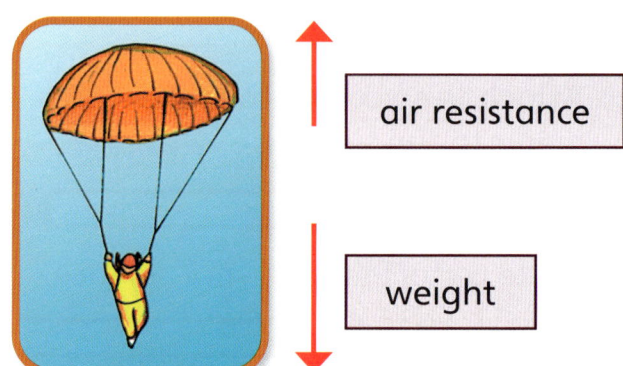

Look at the forces acting on this car.

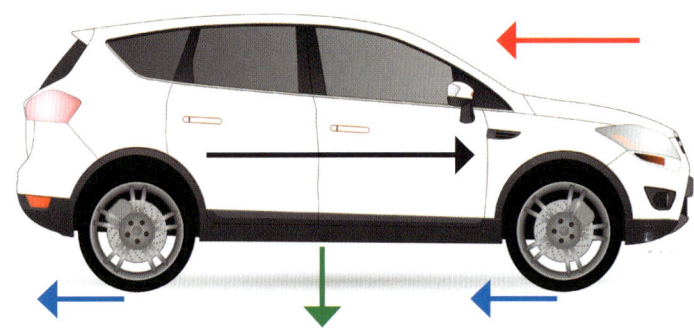

Friction acts between each tyre and the road.
There is also air resistance as the car moves through the air.

The driving force of the car's engine must be equal to, or larger than, these two forces together for the car to move.

Topic 5 | Forces in air and water

Cars are **designed** to reduce friction and air resistance forces.

car from 1930s

car from 2020s

Since the 1930s, the shape of cars has become more **streamlined**. This reduces air resistance.

Which of these boats is more streamlined?

Which is designed for fast speeds?

Now do some **research** yourself.

Choose one of these **sports** to find out more about.
- Ice skating: how do skaters move on the ice?
- Skiing, luge and skeleton: what are the differences between them?
- Curling: why do players brush the ice?

Key words

drag   reduces   parachute   increases   designed

streamlined   research   sports

Investigating streamlining

Streamlined objects are shaped to travel through air or water with as little resistance as possible.

Objects that travel quickly through air or water often have similar **shapes**.

Can you think of any more?

Let's ask a scientific question about this.

Which shape moves **fastest** through liquid?

You will need:
- **modelling clay**
- two identical large plastic bottles
- wallpaper **paste** (or water)
- paper towels.

92

Topic 5 | Forces in air and water

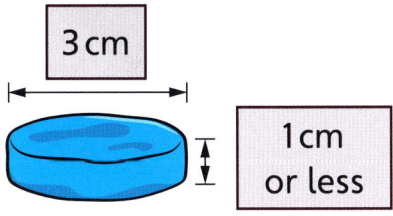

1. Make a flat **disc** with your modelling clay. This size is a guide, it does not need to be exact, but use a whole strip or exactly half a strip of clay to keep the mass of all your shapes the same. This is your '**standard**' to compare with other shapes.

2. Cut the tops off both bottles. Fill them to the same level with wallpaper paste.

3. Make some more shapes that you think will move through the paste *faster* than your standard. Use the same amount of modelling clay as your standard each time.

4. Drop the standard into one bottle and drop one of your shapes into the other bottle at the same time. Keep the starting height you drop them from the same. Don't push or throw the shapes in.

What else should you keep the same?

5. Race each shape in turn against the standard. Wipe paste off the shapes each time.

6. Which shapes were faster than the standard? Race those against each other to find a winner.

7. Now join the rest of the class to find a class winner. Compare them all in the same bottles of paste each time for a fairer test.

Key words

shapes   fastest   modelling clay   paste   disc   standard

93

End of topic questions

Forces in air and water

This is a Winter Olympic sport called **bobsleigh**. It is a team sport in which competitors slide down a narrow, twisting ice track. The fastest team wins.

Discuss your answers to these questions with a partner.

1. How many people are in the bobsleigh?

2. Look at the shape of the bobsleigh. Suggest why it is this shape.

3. The competitors sit down low in the bobsleigh. Suggest why this helps them go faster.

Bobsleighs do not have engines. They just slide downhill.

4. Which force acts on the bobsleigh to pull it down the track?

5. Which forces slow the bobsleigh as it moves?

Topic 5 | End of topic questions

This is a bobsleigh run. It is a metal track covered with ice. The icy surface helps the bobsleighs to go fast.

6 Why will they go faster on ice than on a metal or grassy track?

Competitors start their run outside the bobsleigh. A good start is an important part of the race.

This is a two-person bobsleigh getting ready to go.

Both competitors run on the ice and push the bobsleigh. Then they jump into it. The person at the back jumps in last so that they can stay pushing for longer.

7 Why do their shoes need good grip?

8 Why is the push at the start so important?

9 Why are they wearing smooth clothing?

6 Electricity: changing circuits

> Drawing circuits using symbols makes them easier for everyone to understand. Let's look at some.

You have made simple circuits using bulbs, cells, wires and switches. You have connected motors or buzzers in circuits too.

Electrical circuits are not always simple. Imagine how many wires are connected to make the electrical circuits in a house, office or school.

The learner in the picture is building some circuits. Imagine having to draw complicated circuits as a picture. Scientists have agreed on a set of symbols that everyone can use to represent the components in a circuit. You will be able to use them yourself soon too.

Universal symbols

In Year 4, you made electrical **circuits**. You looked at pictures like this.

How many cells are shown?

How many bulbs are shown?

Why are the bulbs not lit?

In another school, someone may be making circuits from pictures like this.

Find two ways in which this circuit differs from the one above.

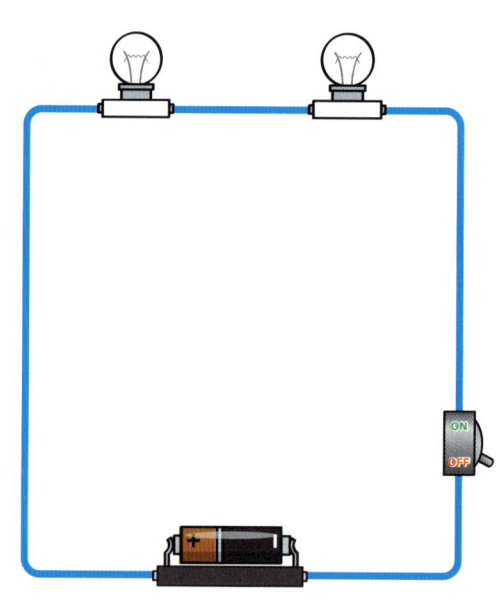

Some scientists use circuits that look like this.

When circuits have several, or many, components in them they are harder to draw.

Even if we do try to draw our circuits, we might do it in different ways. We may not understand the drawings without lots of labels on them.

98

Topic 6 | Electricity: changing circuits

You are familiar with drawing a **diagram** for equipment, like this.

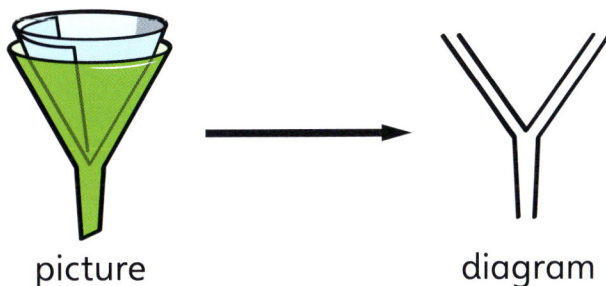

picture → diagram

Scientists draw diagrams for electrical circuits too. Each component has a **symbol**.

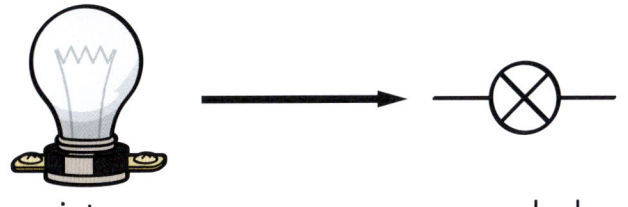

picture → symbol

What is this component?

A symbol is a shape that represents something else. You use symbols in Maths to represent sums.

symbols for numbers

25 + 10 = 35

this symbol tells you to add   this symbol represents 'equals'

The same set of symbols is used by scientists so that everyone can recognise them, whatever language they speak.

It allows scientists to **communicate** quickly in a way that they all understand.

Key words

circuits   symbol   communicate

Circuit symbols

Scientists all use the same symbol for each **component**, so it is important to draw them **accurately**.

These are some of the symbols we use.

Component		Symbol
	one **cell**	—∣⊢—
	two cells (a **battery**)	—∣⊢∣⊢—
	wire	——————
	open **switch**	—o╱o—
	closed switch	—o―o—
	bulb	—⊗—
	buzzer	⏃
	motor	—Ⓜ—

When you are making a circuit, the **switch** is open. So you will use the open switch symbol most often.

100

Look at the symbol for a cell. It is a long, thin line next to a short, slightly wider line, like this.

The horizontal line must touch the vertical line on each side.

You know from Year 4 that a battery is two or more cells joined together.

battery

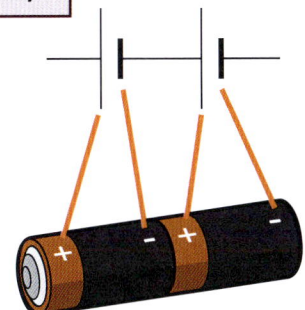

The lines **represent** the + and − ends of each cell.

A battery with cells placed like this would not work.

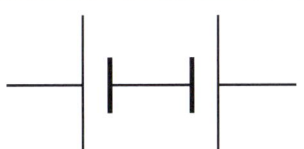

Here is an example of a simple circuit drawn as a picture and as a circuit diagram.

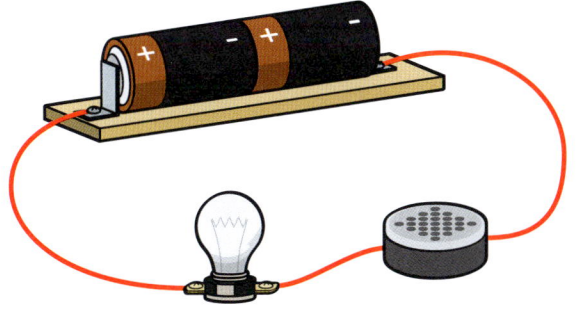
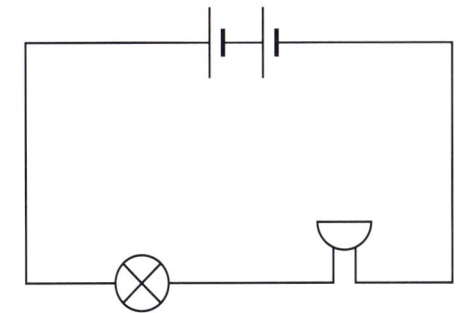

Match each component in the picture to its symbol in the circuit diagram.

Key words

component   accurately   cell   battery   switch   bulb   buzzer

motor   represent

Making circuits

Use some components to make your own circuits.

Work with a partner. You will need:

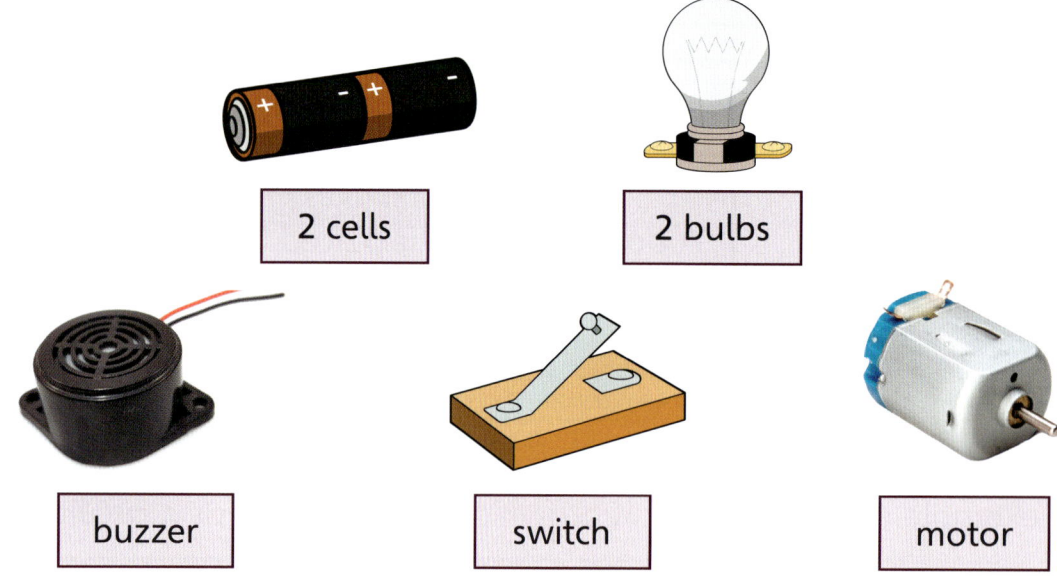

2 cells

2 bulbs

buzzer

switch

motor

1. Make these circuits by looking at the circuit diagrams.

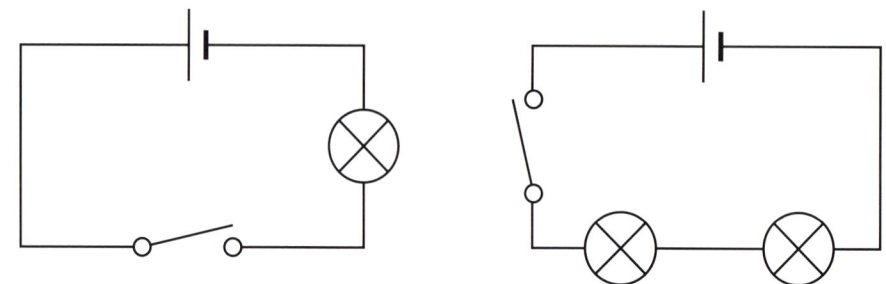

Topic 6 | Electricity: changing circuits

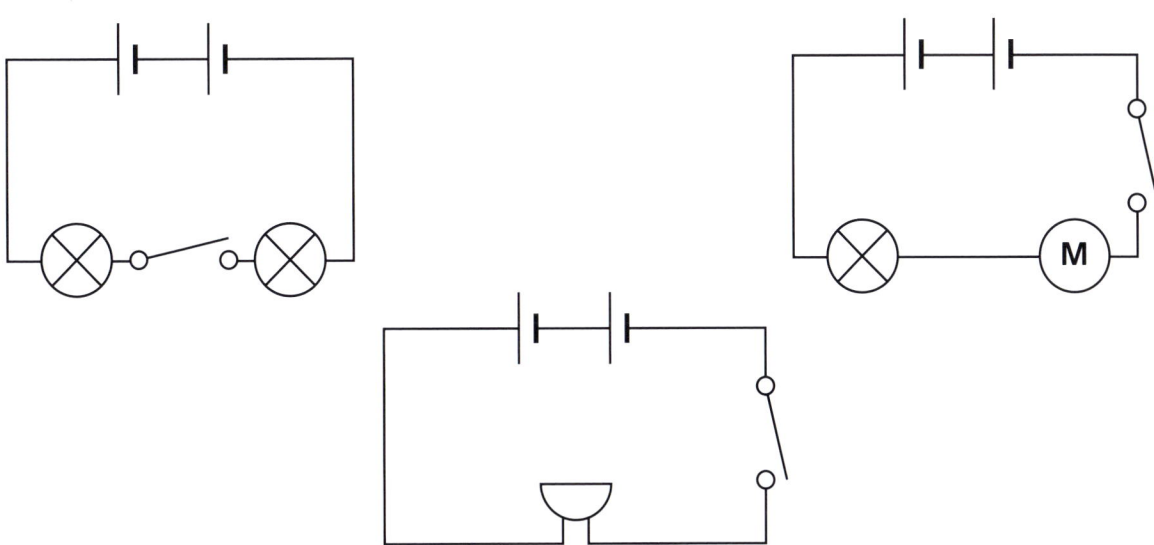

2. Use any of the components to make four different circuits.
   Draw a circuit diagram for each circuit you make.

3. Draw two circuit diagrams for your partner to make.
   Check they are correct.

4. Close your books.
   Can you both draw the symbol for each of these components?
   - cell
   - motor
   - open switch
   - bulb
   - battery
   - buzzer

   Do it by yourselves then **compare** and discuss your answers to check they are correct.

Key words

compare

Investigating how components function

Let's investigate some components in more detail.

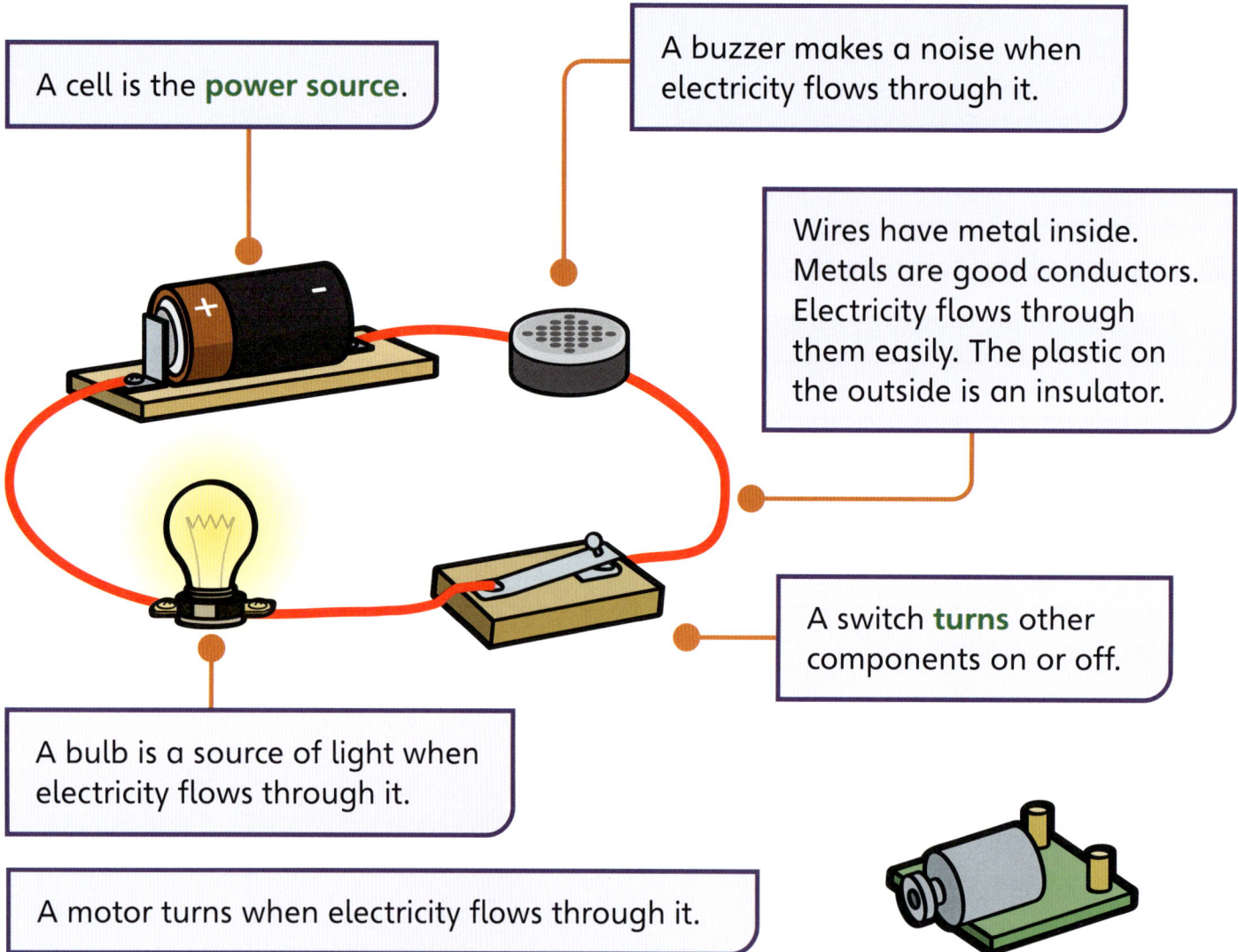

A cell is the **power source**.

A buzzer makes a noise when electricity flows through it.

Wires have metal inside. Metals are good conductors. Electricity flows through them easily. The plastic on the outside is an insulator.

A switch **turns** other components on or off.

A bulb is a source of light when electricity flows through it.

A motor turns when electricity flows through it.

Components need electricity from the cell to work. Electricity does not flow through them as easily as it does through the wires. The more components there are, the smaller the share of electricity they receive.

Topic 6 | Electricity: changing circuits

Now make these circuits.

1.

Can you see the difference in **brightness**?

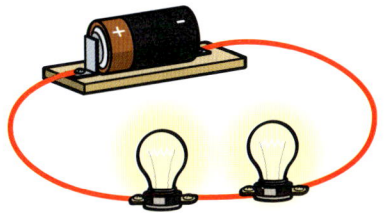

Can you see the dim light?

2.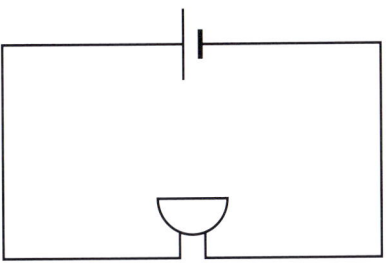

How can you make the buzzer louder? Try it.

Think of a way of making the buzzer quieter, but not silent. Try it.

3.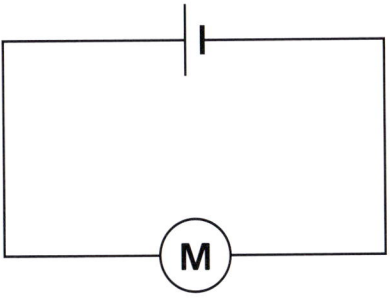

How can you make the motor turn faster? Try it.

Think of two different ways to make the motor turn more slowly. Try them.

Key words

power source   turns   brightness

105

Make a windmill

Switches break a circuit. The other components only work when there is a **complete circuit.**

Closing the switch completes the circuit so electricity can flow around it.

Use a motor and a switch to make an object that has moving parts. A windmill is an example, but you could design your own.

You will need:
- one or two motors
- a switch
- a cell
- **connecting wires**
- other materials such as cardboard, an empty milk carton or plastic bottle
- glue and scissors.

Here are some ideas to help you design a windmill.

Topic 6 | Electricity: changing circuits

Use this circuit if you have one windmill ...

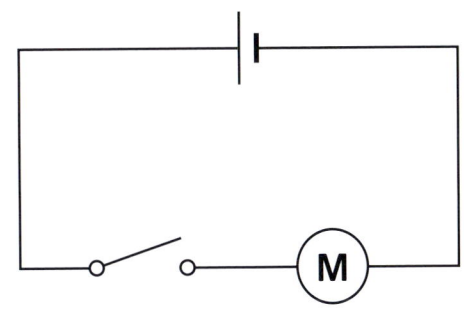

... or this circuit for two smaller ones together.

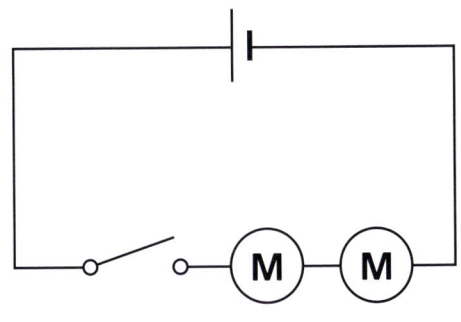

You may need a second cell in this circuit.

The motor and cell can be hidden at the back of the windmill, or inside it.

Put the switch in a place where you can turn it on and off easily.

Think of one way you could improve your windmill if you made it again.

Can you think of other devices that use a motor?

Could you make a working model of any of them?

Key words

complete circuit   connecting wires

End of topic activity

Electricity: changing circuits

Try making a quiz board.

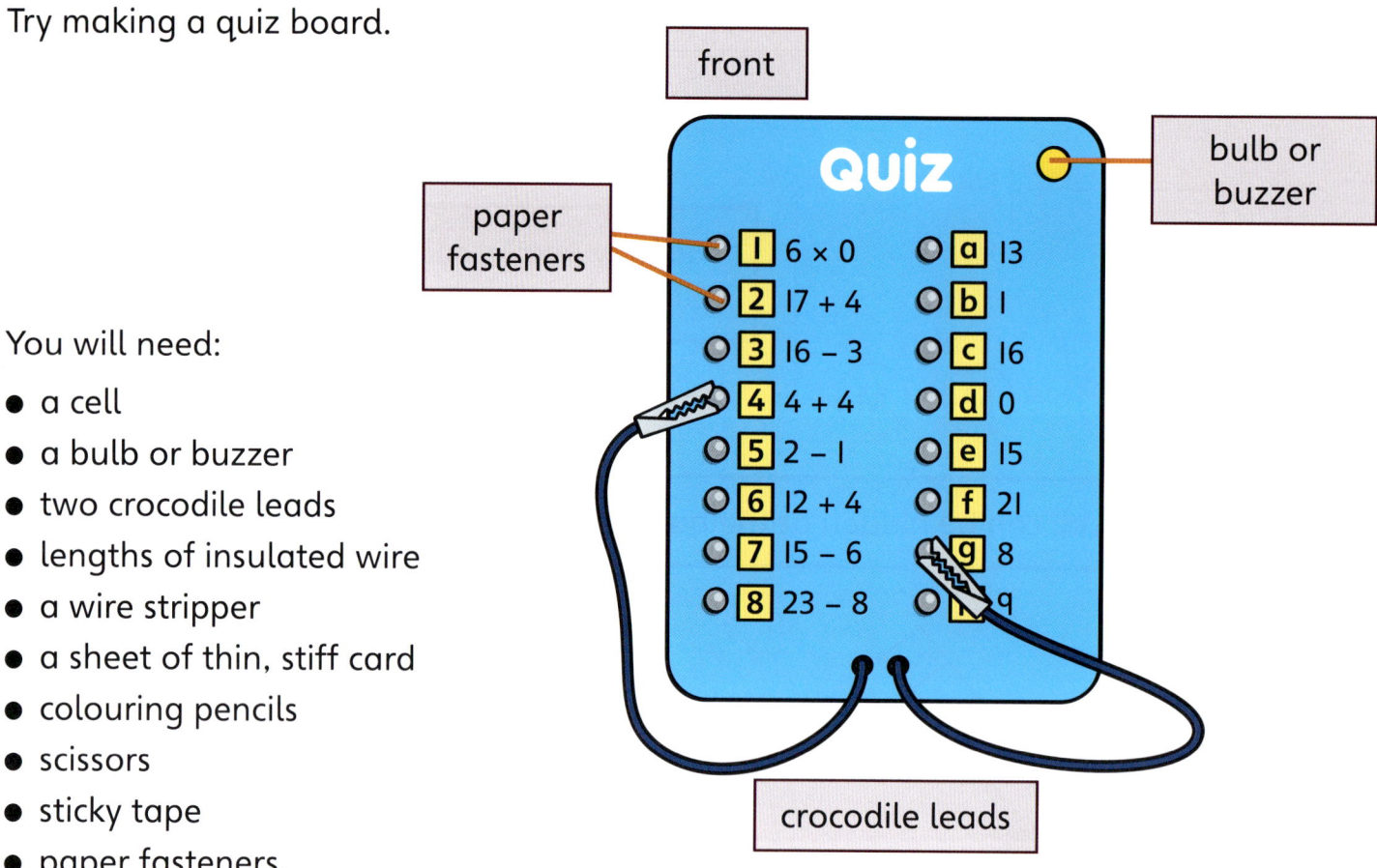

You will need:
- a cell
- a bulb or buzzer
- two crocodile leads
- lengths of insulated wire
- a wire stripper
- a sheet of thin, stiff card
- colouring pencils
- scissors
- sticky tape
- paper fasteners.

Do not try this with any power source other than the one your teacher gives you.

1. Write your questions and answers on the card. Put questions on the left and the answers, jumbled up, on the right.

2. Push one paper fastener through the card beside every question and every answer.

3. Make two holes for the crocodile leads to go through.

4. Ask an adult to help you choose the correct wire length and to show you how to strip about 2 cm of insulation from each end.

Topic 6 | End of topic questions

5 Use your lengths of wire to join the correct questions and answers together by wrapping it around the paper fastener on the back of the card. Hold it in place with a piece of tape over it.

6 Now connect your circuit components and check the circuit works by touching the two crocodile leads together.

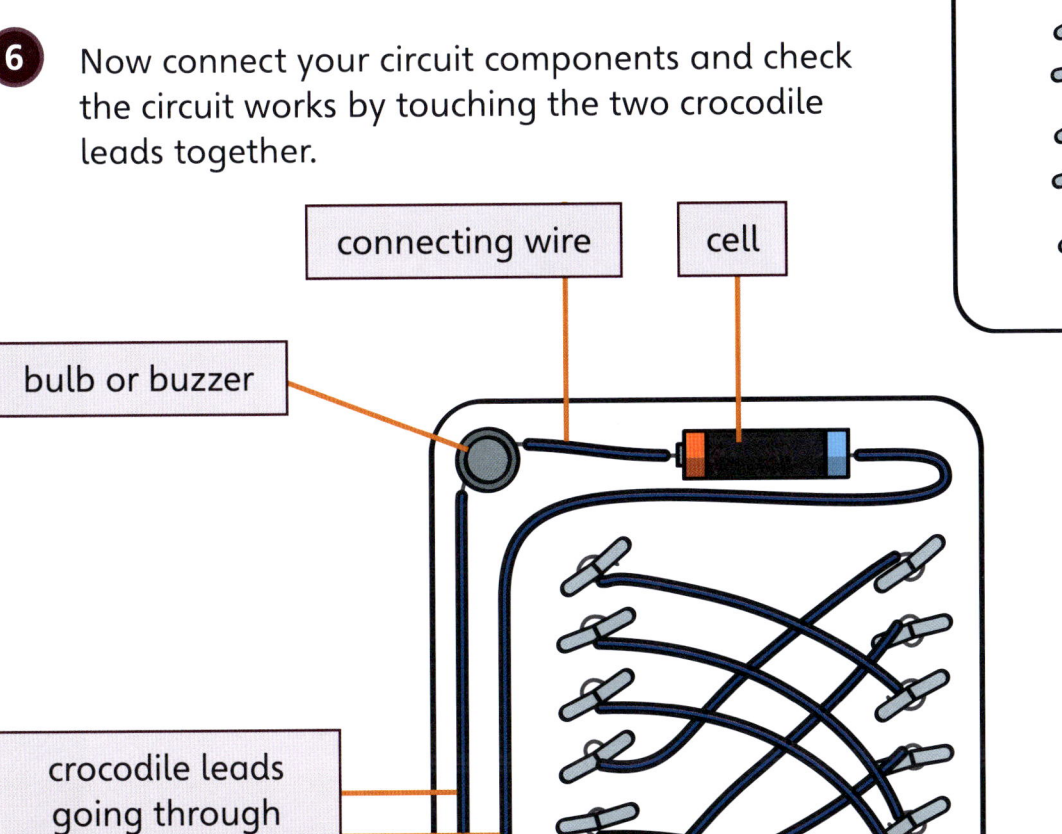

7 Touch the tip of one crocodile lead onto the paper fastener beside a question. Touch the other lead on the correct answer. The bulb or buzzer should let you know that you are correct.

8 Now see if your partner can answer all your questions correctly. Can you answer theirs correctly too?

7 Revision

You have reached the end of the new topics. Let's look at some of the things you need to know for the Year 6 examination.

You know a lot of science now. You know lots of new words with precise meanings.

This section of the book contains all the topics that are tested in the end of Year 6 examination.

The learner in the picture has made some notes about each topic he has to learn about. Now he is reading through them. This is a good thing to do to start your preparation. It is also important to **do** some things to **test** your knowledge. You should check what you know, and what you do not know, in order to improve. If you were learning to play football, you might read the rules of the game first, but you soon need to go and play the game to find out what you are able to do. Then you can work on the things that you are not so good at … or ask for help.

Learning things for an examination is like that too. Until you check what you know, and what you do not know, then it is hard to improve. Keep talking to other learners – you may be able to help them, and they may be able to help you too.

Feeding relationships

Revision topic 1

Here are some key points for this topic.

- All living things need food.
- The availability of food affects the size of animal populations and where they can live.
- Plants make their own food.
- Animals depend on plants, other animals or both for their food.

Here are some important definitions.

producer	a living thing in a food chain that can make its own food For example, plants are producers. They are at the start of food chains.
consumer	an animal in a food chain that eats another living thing
predator	an animal that hunts other animals to eat
prey	an animal that is hunted by other animals
herbivore	an animal that eats plants
carnivore	an animal that eats other animals

Topic 7 | Revision

Here are some key things to understand and to be able to do.

■ Draw and answer questions about food chains

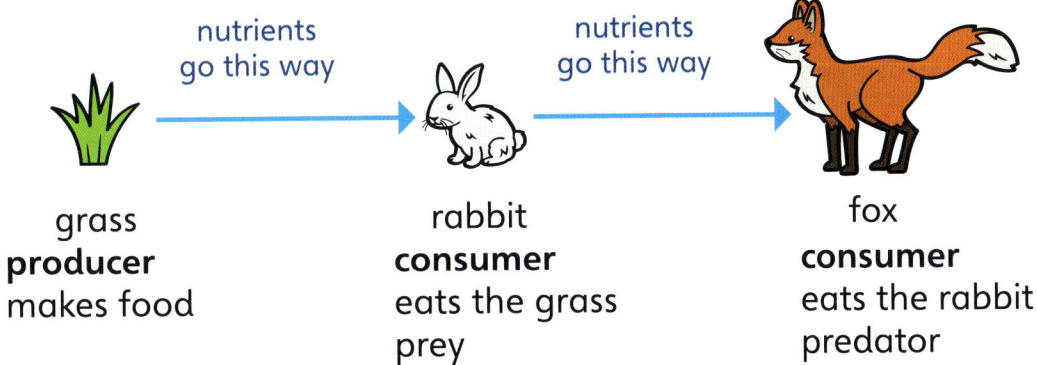

The fox is a predator of the rabbit. The rabbit is the fox's prey.

grass ⟶ rabbit ⟶ fox ⟶ eagle

The eagle is a predator of the fox. The fox is the eagle's prey.

■ Identify producers, consumers, herbivores, carnivores, predators and prey in food chains and food webs

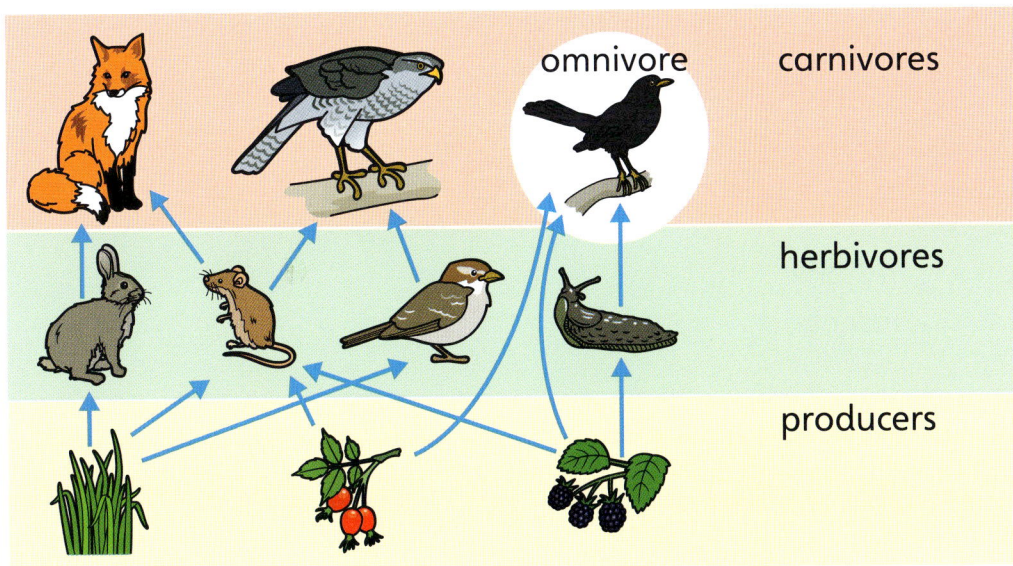

The blackbird is an omnivore. It eats plants and animals. The blackbird is a predator of the slug. The slug is its prey.

Can you see two more predators? Which animals are their prey?

Variation and classification

Revision topic 2

Here are some key points for this topic.

- Living things are classified into groups using features that we observe.
- To classify living things, scientists look at their similarities and differences.

- Vertebrates have a backbone; invertebrates do not.
- There are five vertebrate groups:
  - mammals, birds, reptiles, amphibians and fish.
- There are more invertebrate groups.
- Examples of some invertebrate groups are:
  - slugs and snails
  - worms
  - crabs
  - spiders
  - insects.

- Plants can be flowering or non-flowering.
- Flowering plants include grasses and trees.
- Non-flowering plants include ferns and mosses.

Topic 7 | Revision

Here are some key things to understand and to be able to do.

■ **Identify and use observable features to classify a specific plant or animal**

This buttercup flower has 5 shiny yellow petals.

Each green leaf has serrated edges.

Earthworms are invertebrates. They are usually pink, brown or red in colour.

They have a long, thin body divided into many segments. They burrow in moist soil. They can sense light but they do not have eyes.

■ **Use a key to identify living things**

Use the key to identify these flowers.

A   B   C   D

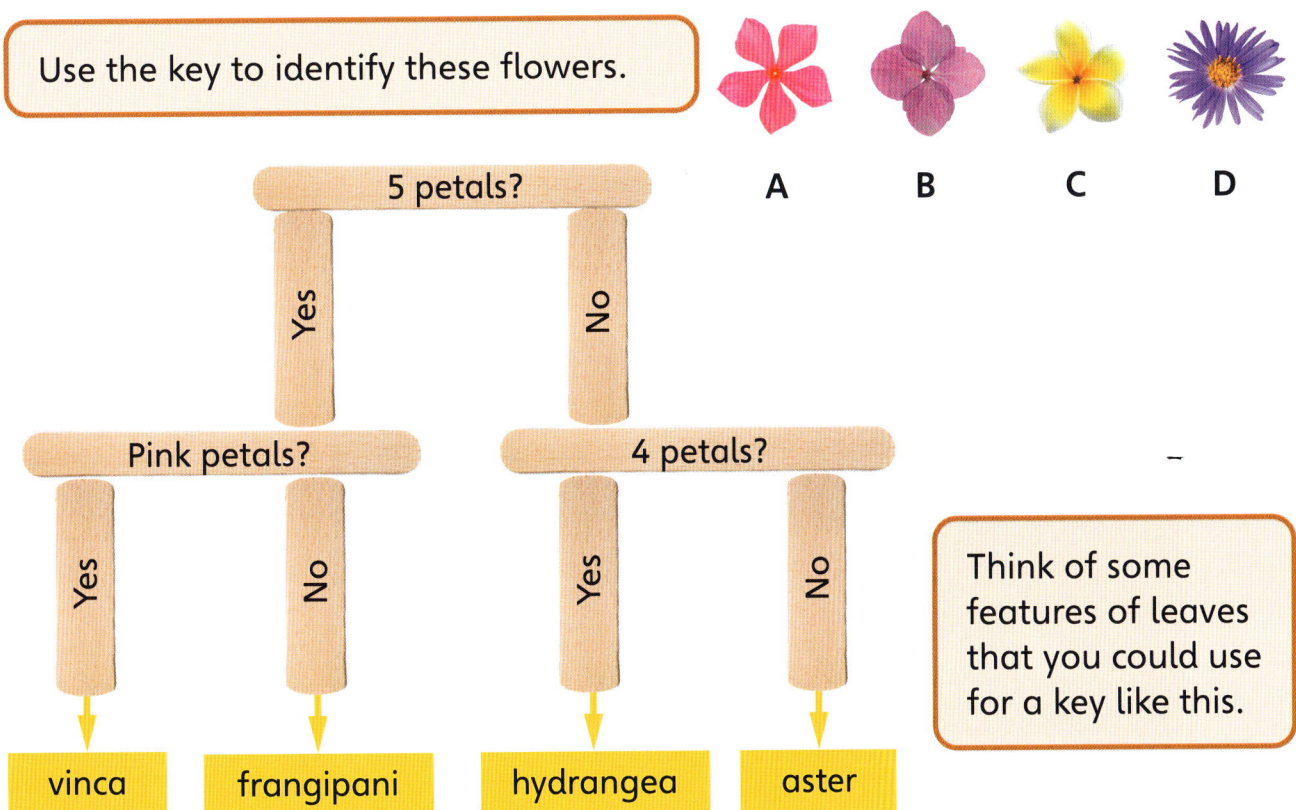

Think of some features of leaves that you could use for a key like this.

Growing plants

Revision topic 3

Here are some key points for this topic.

- Plants need the correct amount of water and light to grow well.
- Soil provides minerals to help plants grow.
- Fertilisers and organic matter can give plants extra minerals.

Here are some key things to understand and to be able to do.

■ **Understand how water is transported inside plants**

air

③ Water evaporates from the leaves.

② Water moves up the stem to the leaves.

water

① Roots take in water from the soil.

When water evaporates from the leaves into the air, more water moves up the stem.

Topic 7 | Revision

■ **Recognise parts of a plant on a diagram and know their functions**

This is a sunflower plant.   This is a tree.

A tree has a trunk. Other flowering plants have a stem.

Part of plant	Function
roots	anchor the plant
	take in water and minerals
stem or trunk	supports the plant
	transports water and nutrients (such as minerals an food the plant makes)
leaves	make food using sunlight for nutrition
flowers	attract insects for pollination
	make seeds for reproduction

How would you describe the difference between a stem and a trunk?

What is the word that describes living things that make their own food?

117

Plant adaptations

Revision topic 4

Here are some key points for this topic.

- Different habitats and microhabitats have different environmental conditions.
- Temperature, light and water are examples of environmental conditions.
- Environmental conditions can bring about variation (differences) between living things of the same species.

 water

- The availability of water may affect the pattern of plant root growth.

 light

- Plants need light to make their food.
- The availability of light affects the growth and size of plants.
- The availability of light affects where plants can live and grow.

Topic 7 | Revision

Here are some key things to understand and to be able to do.

■ **Understand ways in which plants are suited to their environment**

How are these plants suited to their habitat?

■ **Predict the likely habitat of plants from the adaptations they show**

What adaptations do these plants show?
What sort of habitat do they live in?

■ **Compare features of plant adaptations in two contrasting habitats**

Compare these plants.

freshwater pond rainforest

Micro-organisms

Revision topic 5

Here are some key points for this topic.

- Micro-organisms are so small that we need a microscope to see them.
- Micro-organisms can be bacteria, viruses or microscopic fungi, for example yeasts.
- The table shows how to use these words.

one	many
bacterium	bacteria
virus	viruses
fungus	fungi

- Micro-organisms growing and reproducing on food can cause food poisoning.
- Bacteria and fungi are involved in the process of decay.
- Breaking down dead animals and plant material releases nutrients, such as minerals, back to the soil.

Here are some key things to understand and to be able to do.

■ **Know ways in which micro-organisms can be harmful**

Bacteria, viruses and microscopic fungi cause diseases. Mould fungi spoil food as they grow and feed on it.

causing disease
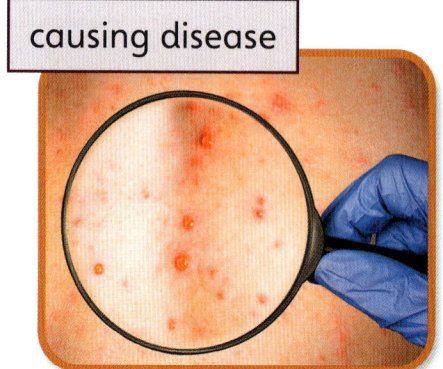

food going mouldy

mould

food poisoning

■ **Explain some food hygiene precautions to reduce the risk of food poisoning**

Wash hands before touching food.

Clean surfaces.

Refrigerate fresh food.

Keep flies and other insects away from food.

Take extra care when preparing food for other people.

■ **Know ways in which micro-organisms can be useful**

Yeast makes bread dough rise.

Bacteria change milk to yoghurt.

making cheeses

making compost

Bacteria change milk from a liquid to a solid.

Fungi can add new tastes and colours to cheese.

Bacteria and fungi are decomposers. They break down dead animals and plant material and release their nutrients for living plants to use from the soil.

Plant life cycles

Revision topic 6

Here are some key points for this topic.

- Some plants have flowers that produce seeds, which grow into new plants.

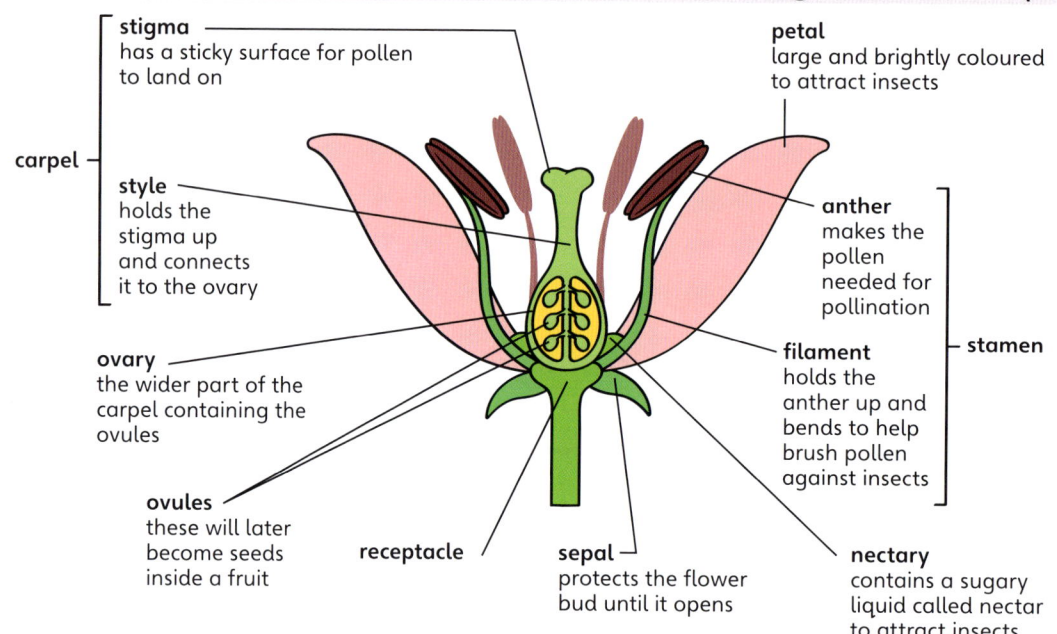

- Pollination is the transfer of pollen from the anther to the stigma on the same or a different flower.
- Fertilisation occurs when material from inside the pollen (its nucleus) combines with the nucleus in an ovule.
- Germination is when a seed starts to grow into a new plant.
- Seeds need water, oxygen from the air and the correct temperature to germinate.
- A plant life cycle involves germination, flowering, pollination, fertilisation and seed dispersal, in that order.
- Seeds need to be dispersed so that they grow in new places and are not in competition with the parent plant.
- Seeds can be dispersed in different ways, e.g. water, wind, animals or exploding pods.

Topic 7 | Revision

Here are some important definitions.

■ **Explain the function of the parts of an insect-pollinated flower**

Part of flower	Function
sepals	protect the flower bud until it opens
petals	large and brightly coloured to attract insects
nectary	contains a sugary liquid called nectar to attract insects
anther	makes the pollen needed for pollination
filament	holds the anther up and bends to help brush pollen against insects
stigma	has a sticky surface for pollen to land on
style	holds the stigma up and connects it to the ovary
ovary	the wider part of the carpel containing the ovules; the ovary later becomes a fruit
ovules	these will later become seeds inside a fruit

■ **Compare the processes of insect and wind pollination**

Insect pollination	Wind pollination
bright flowers with large, coloured petals and nectar	small, green flowers
short filaments so stamens are inside flower	long filaments so anthers hang outside flower
insects brush against sticky pollen	wind blows small, light pollen
pollen from insects sticks to the stigma	long feathery stigmas catch wind-blown pollen

Heart, lungs and circulation

Revision topic 7

Here are some key points for this topic.

- The circulatory system is the heart and blood vessels that contain blood.
- The heart is an organ that pumps blood.
- Blood transports water and nutrients around our bodies.
- Pulse rate is a measure of how fast the heart is pumping blood.
- Pulse rate is measured in beats per minute (bpm).

- The lungs are in the thorax.
- Lungs are the organs used for breathing.
- Air is a mixture of gases, including oxygen.
- Blood picks up oxygen from the lungs.
- Oxygen is transported through blood vessels to organs of the body.

Here are some important definitions.

breathing	ventilation of the lungs to move air in and out
respiration	how the body uses oxygen when it reaches all the organs

Topic 7 | Revision

Here are some key things to understand and to be able to do.

■ **Understand how pulse rate changes with exercise**

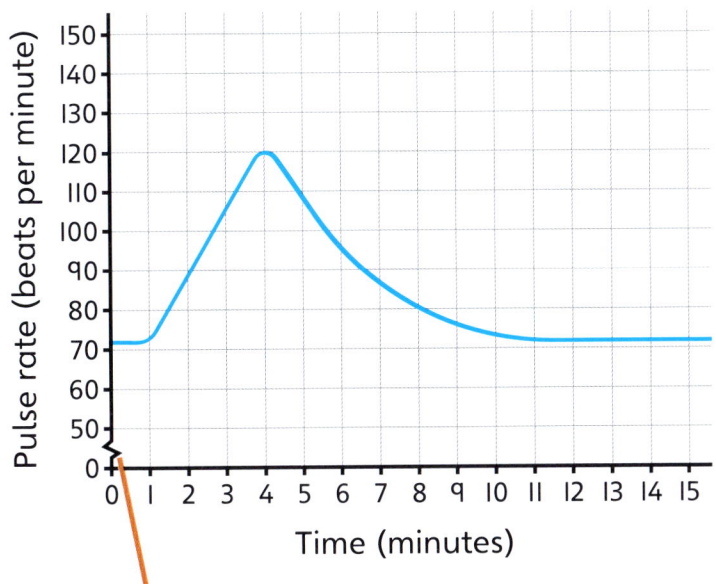

Pulse rate increases rapidly at the start of exercise.

Pulse rate decreases more slowly after exercise. It then returns to the resting pulse rate.

Find out what this means.

How long was the exercise?

What was the highest pulse rate? What is the resting pulse rate?

■ **Explain the reason for a change in pulse rate during exercise**

During exercise, muscles need more oxygen and nutrients for respiration. This gives them energy to contract.

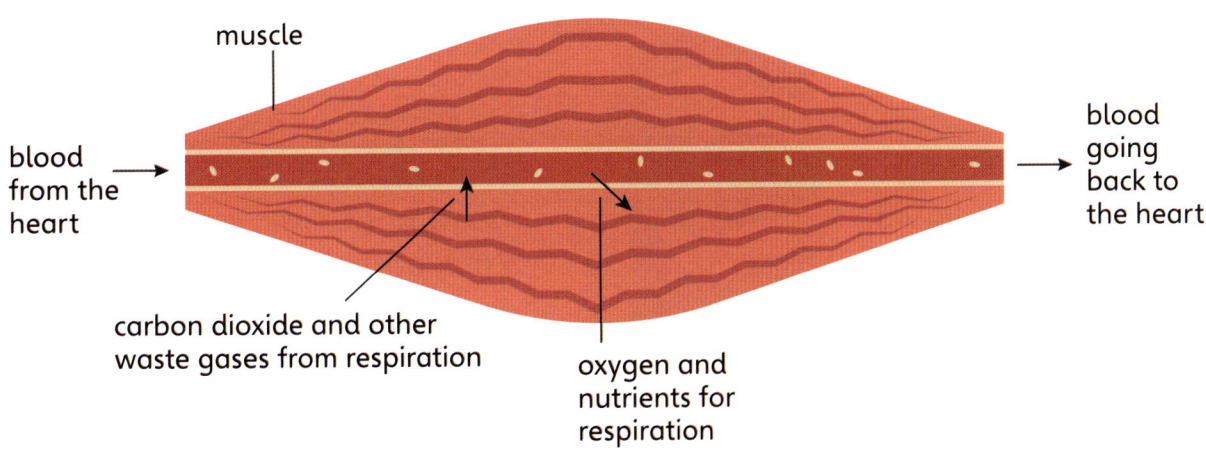

Solids, liquids and gases

Revision topic 8

Here are some key points for this topic.

- Temperature is a measure of how hot or cold something is.
- Temperature is measured in degrees Celsius (°C) using a thermometer.
- Water exists in three states, and changes from one to another at different temperatures.
- Different substances change state at different temperatures.

- Solids hold their shape and do not flow.
- Liquids flow and form a pool or take the shape of their container.
- Gases move easily and escape from a container if the lid is taken off.
- Solids made of very small particles, like sand, sugar and salt, can behave like liquids in some ways.

Here are some key things to understand and to be able to do.

■ **Understand these properties of sand, sugar and salt**

This sand is a solid. It flows like a liquid.

It makes a pile, not a pool. Each grain is a tiny solid.

Topic 7 | Revision

■ **Identify substances as solids, liquids and gases and know the differences between them**

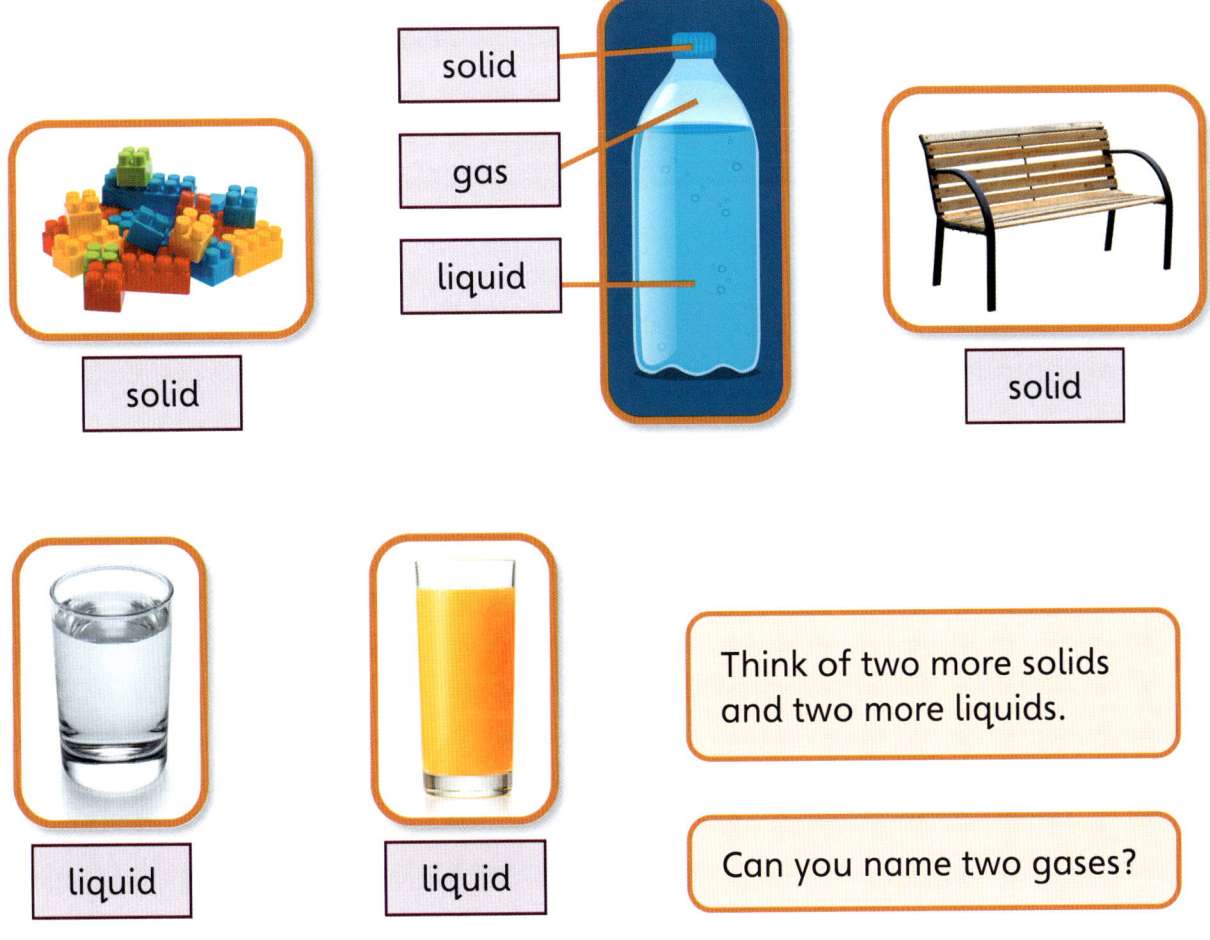

Think of two more solids and two more liquids.

Can you name two gases?

Here are some properties of liquids.

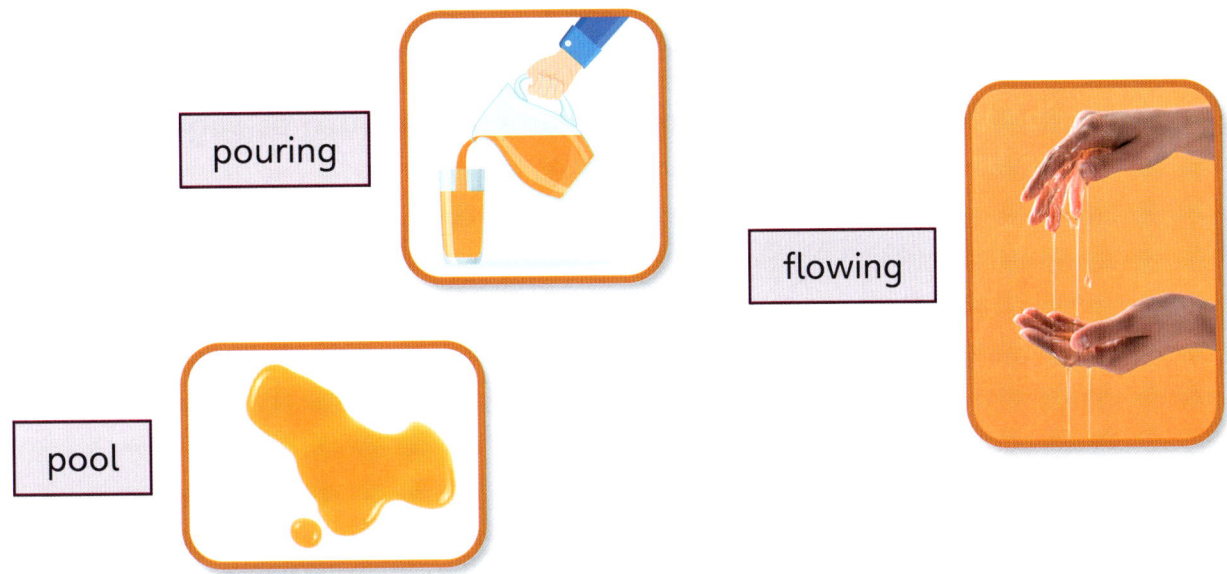

Mixing and separating materials

Revision topic 9

Here are some key points for this topic.

- Solids can be mixed to form a mixture.
- Sieving may be used to separate some mixtures.
- Some mixtures can be separated using a magnet.
- Filtration may be used to separate some mixtures.
- Liquids pass through the filter paper; insoluble solids do not.
- Sand and flour are insoluble solids that can be separated by filtration.

- When a solid dissolves in water, it forms a solution that cannot be separated by filtration.
- Sugar and salt are soluble solids.
- When a solution is left exposed to air the liquid evaporates into the air and the dissolved solid stays in the dish.

Here are some key things to understand and to be able to do.

■ Describe the ways in which soluble substances such as sugar and salt can be dissolved more quickly

crush the solid

heat the liquid

stir the mixture

Topic 7 | Revision

■ **Suggest ways in which different mixtures can be separated**

- If one material is magnetic, use a magnet.
- If two solids have grains of different sizes, use a sieve.
- If there is an insoluble solid in a liquid, use filtration.
- If there is a dissolved solid in a liquid, use evaporation.

■ **Describe or answer questions about tables and graphs that show how much of different solids dissolve in the same volume of water**

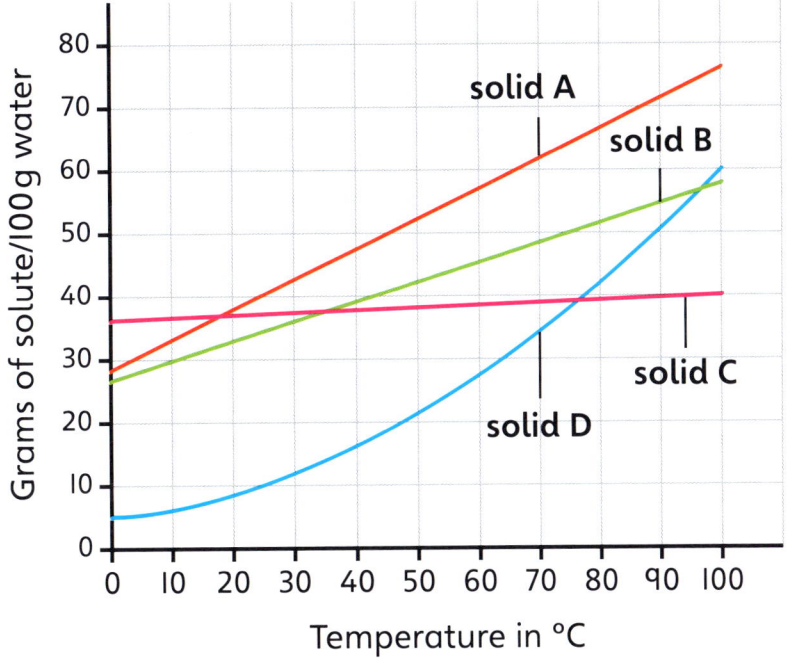

How much of **solid C** dissolved at 90 °C?

At what temperature did 10 g of **solid D** dissolve?

Think of two questions you could ask your partner about **solid A** and **solid B**.

Reversible and irreversible change

Revision topic 10

Here are some key points for this topic.

- Some mixtures can be separated using sieving, filtration or magnetism.
- A solute can be separated from a solution by evaporating the solvent.

- Melting, freezing, evaporation and condensation are changes of state.
- Changes of state need changes of temperature.

Red arrows show heating.
Blue arrows show cooling.

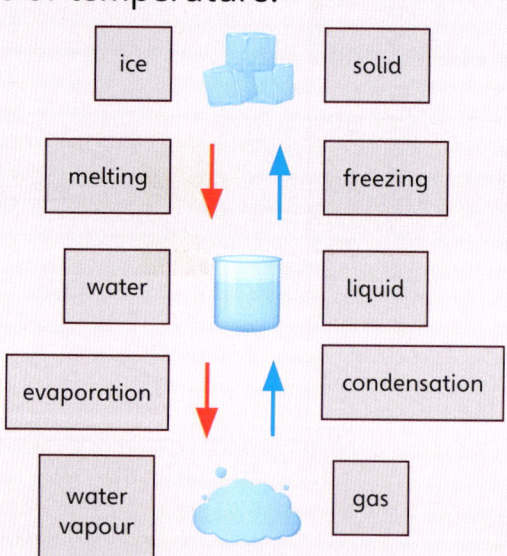

- Dissolving, mixing and changes of state are reversible.
- Some changes cause new materials to form; this kind of change is not usually reversible.
- When an acid, such as vinegar, and bicarbonate of soda are mixed, heat and bubbles of gas are evidence that new materials have formed.

Topic 7 | Revision

Here are some key things to understand and to be able to do.

- **Understand the terms dissolving, solution, solvent and solute**

- **Understand evaporation and condensation in the water cycle**

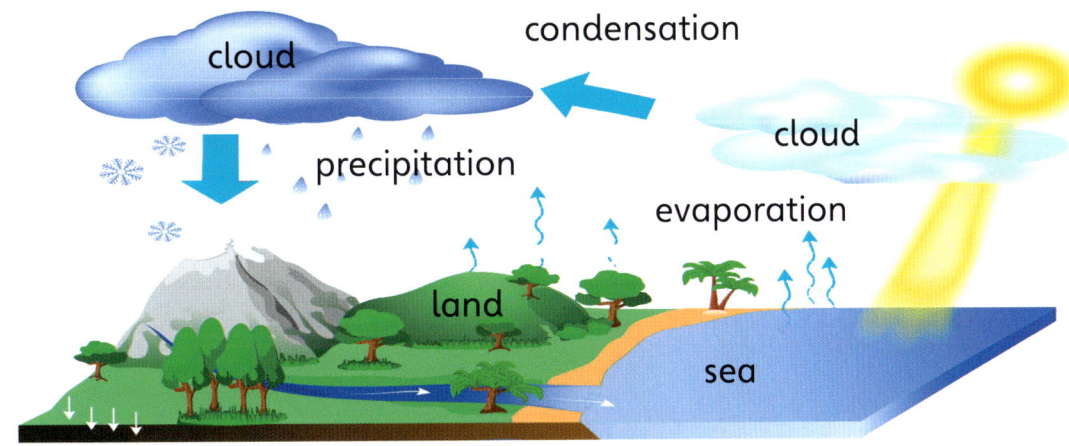

- **Choose methods of separating any combination of these materials**

sugar	sand	small pieces of iron	pebbles
salt	flour	rice grains	stones

Which of these materials is magnetic?

- **Know about some simple irreversible changes**

iron nail rusting

wood burning

bread cooking

Light

Revision topic 11

Here are some key points for this topic.

- We need light to be able to see things.
- Dark is the absence of light.

- Some materials block light.
- Materials that block light are described as being opaque.

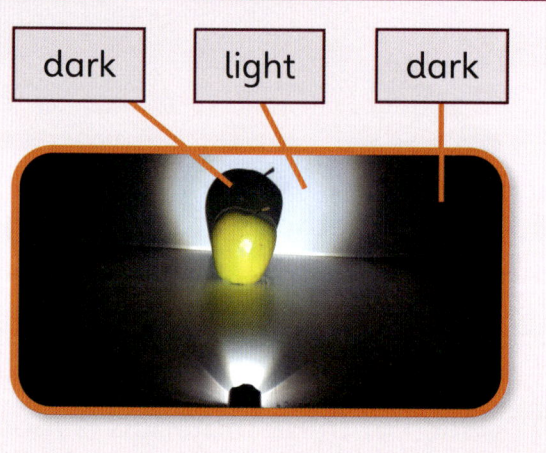

- A shadow is formed when light from a source is blocked by an opaque object.
- The shadow is the same shape as the opaque object.
- The position of a shadow is affected by the position of the opaque object.

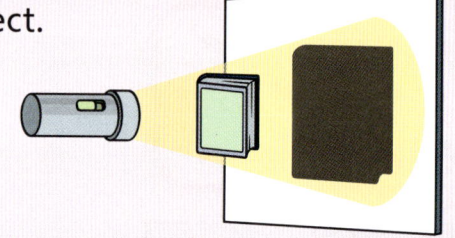

Topic 7 | Revision

Here are some key things to understand and to be able to do.

■ **Understand patterns in the way that the size of shadows changes**

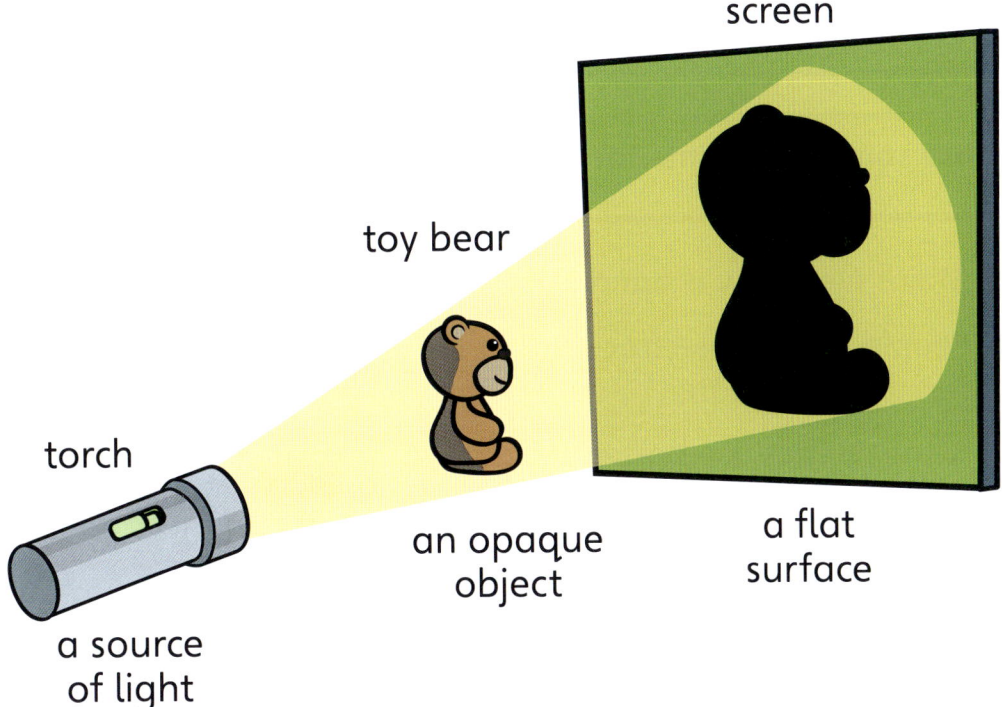

Moving the toy bear nearer to the torch makes the shadow bigger.
Moving the toy bear further from the torch makes the shadow smaller.

■ **Be able to describe patterns using words ending in -er**

The nearer the opaque object is to the light source, the bigger the shadow.
The further the opaque object is from the light source, the smaller the shadow.

Electricity: everyday uses and simple circuits

Revision topic 12

Here are some key points for this topic.

- Mains electricity is dangerous.
- People may be electrocuted, or fires may start, when electricity is not used with care.
- Some devices use batteries, which supply electricity.

- A circuit needs a power source to work.
- A complete circuit is needed for a device to work.
- A switch can be used to break a circuit.
- Some materials, such as copper, conduct electricity well; these are electrical conductors.
- Other materials, such as plastic, do not conduct electricity well; these are electrical insulators.

Here are some key things to understand and to be able to do.

■ **Understand some uses of electricity and identify common appliances that use electricity**

Think of some kitchen appliances that use electricity.

Think of an appliance that produces:
- heat
- light
- sound
- movement
- heat and light
- light and sound.

Topic 7 | Revision

■ **Identify these things in simple circuits**

Connection errors

The bulb does not light.

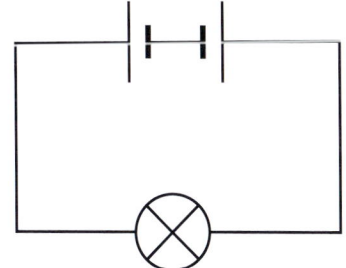

Both + signs must face the **same** way.

Open and closed switches

There is an incomplete circuit.

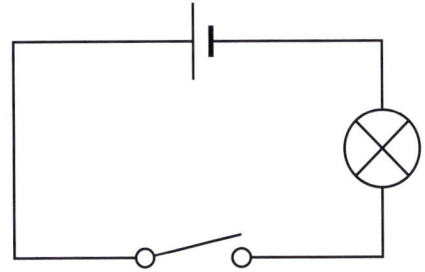

Effect of components breaking

If bulb A breaks, the circuit is no longer complete so bulb B cannot light either.

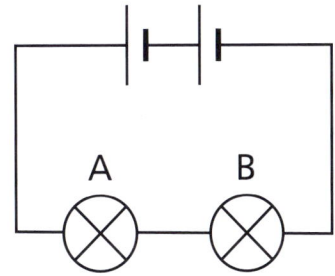

■ **Understand how electrical conductors and insulators are used in electrical cables and household appliances**

Find materials here that are conductors.

Which are insulators? Why are insulators needed?

135

Seeing and reflecting

Revision topic 13

Here are some key points for this topic.

- Light comes from a source.

- Light appears to travel in straight lines.

- Some objects that are **not** light sources can reflect light.

- Light can be reflected from a shiny surface.
- When light is reflected, it changes direction.
- Smooth and shiny surfaces reflect light better than dull surfaces.

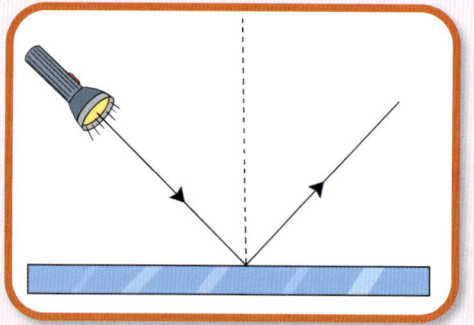

Here are some key definitions for this topic.

opaque	an opaque object blocks light
translucent	translucent materials let some light through; you cannot see clearly through them
transparent	transparent materials let lots of light through; you can see things very clearly through them

Topic 7 | Revision

Here are some key things to understand and to be able to do.

- **Identify sources of light**

Can you name the sources of light on the opposite page?

Can you name two more?

- **Explain that we see things because light travels from light sources into our eyes**

Represent this with a ray diagram like this.

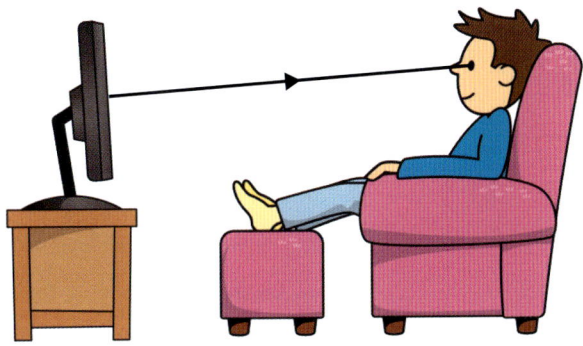

- **Explain that we also see things because light travels from light sources to objects and then into our eyes**

Are you confident that you can draw or complete this sort of ray diagram?

Practise drawing some ray diagrams. Remember to use a ruler.

137

Electricity: changing circuits

Revision topic 14

Here are some key points for this topic.

- Scientists use symbols for circuit components so that everyone can understand what they mean.

Component		Symbol
	one cell	—|⊢—
	two cells (a battery)	—|⊢|⊢—
	wire	———
	open switch	—o/ o—
	closed switch	—o—o—
	bulb	—⊗—
	buzzer	⊔
	motor	—Ⓜ—

Practise drawing these symbols.
Work with a partner to test each other.

Topic 7 | Revision

Here are some key things to understand and to be able to do.

■ **Explain that what happens to components in a circuit is affected by different factors**

1. More cells, or higher voltage cells, make bulbs brighter.

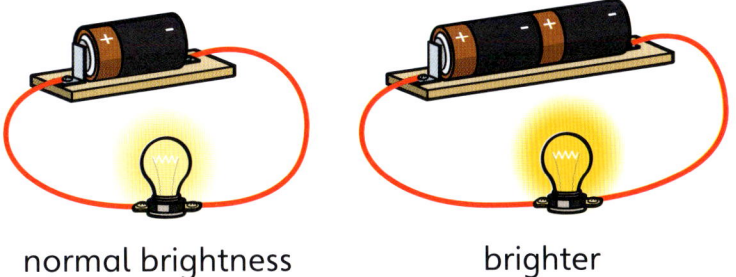

normal brightness   brighter

2. More cells, or higher voltage cells, make buzzers sound louder and motors turn faster.

3. Adding more bulbs, buzzers or motors to a circuit makes bulbs dimmer, buzzers quieter and motors turn more slowly.

4. A switch can make a gap in the circuit. It is used to turn other components on and off.

5. If one bulb breaks, the other bulb will not light. There is now an incomplete circuit.

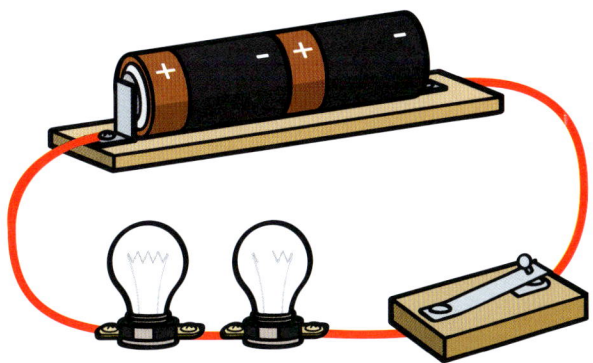

Now read through numbers 1 to 3 again, but say 'fewer' or 'lower' every time you see 'more' or 'higher'.

Can you describe the correct effect this new change will have?

Earth and space

Revision topic 15

Here are some key points for this topic.

- Earth, the Sun and the Moon are part of the Solar System.
- The Sun is a star at the centre of our Solar System.

- Earth is a planet with one moon.
- Planets have different sizes.
- Some planets have more than one moon.
- Earth and other planets orbit the Sun.
- The Moon orbits Earth.

- Earth spins on its axis causing:
  - some parts of Earth to be in daylight when other parts are in darkness
  - shadow lengths to change during the course of a day.
- Earth's rotation makes us think that the Sun is moving across the sky, but it is not.

Topic 7 | Revision

Here are some key things to understand and to be able to do.

■ **Know the eight planets and their positions relative to each other and the Sun**

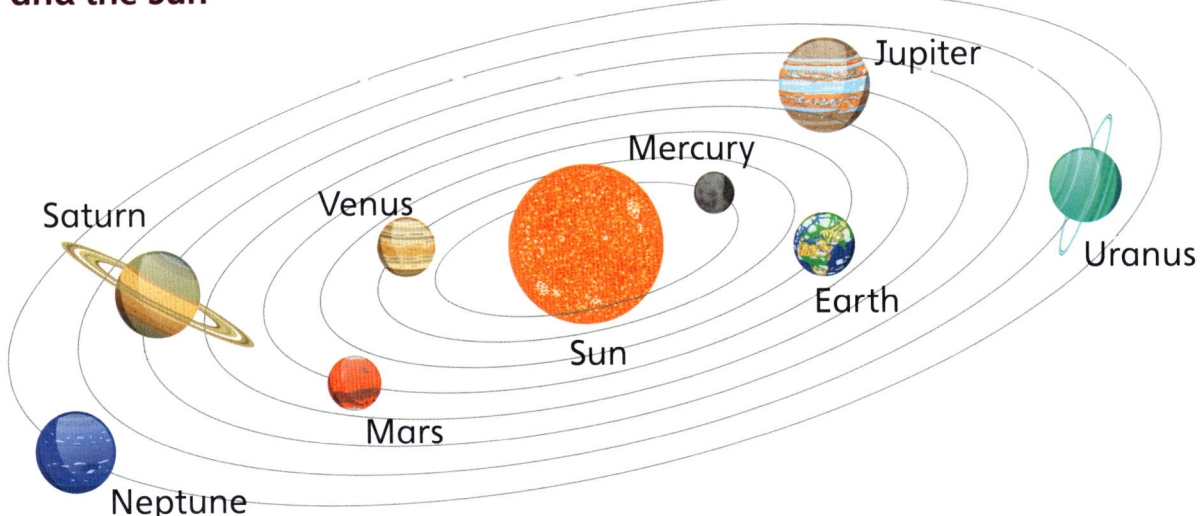

■ **Understand that ideas about the Solar System have changed and developed over time**

Copernicus' later heliocentric model had the Sun at the centre.

Ptolemy's geocentric model had Earth at the centre.

improvements in equipment, observations and information (data)

Which planets had not been discovered?

Compare these two models.

141

Forces in air and water

Revision topic 16

Here are some key points for this topic.

- Objects fall towards the Earth.
- The force of gravity acts between Earth and the falling object.
- Weight is a force.

- Forces are measured in newtons (N).
- More than one force can act on an object at the same time.
- Forces can be represented by the direction and size of an arrow.
- Forces may be balanced or unbalanced; this affects the direction or the motion of an object, or both.

- Friction is a force that acts on moving objects to slow them down.
- Friction can act between solid surfaces and air.
- Friction can also act between solid surfaces and water.
- Air resistance and water resistance are forces that reduce the speed of moving objects.
- Air resistance and water resistance slow streamlined objects less than objects that are not streamlined.
- Streamlining, smoothing surfaces and using oil are ways to reduce the effects of friction.

Topic 7 | Revision

Here are some key things to understand and to be able to do.

■ **Identify where forces are balanced or unbalanced**

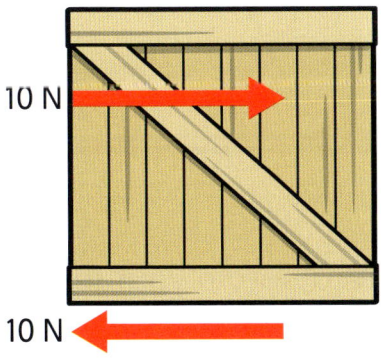
balanced forces
the object does not move

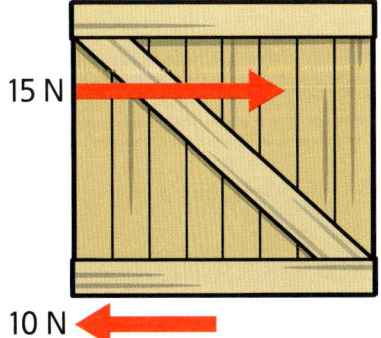
unbalanced forces
the object moves

■ **Describe ways that friction is useful**

Friction can be used to affect how well an object grips a surface.

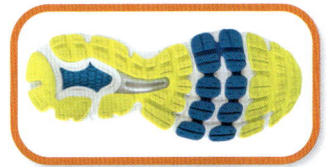

This pavement surface helps to improve grip.

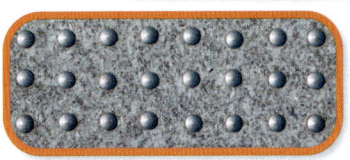

■ **Describe ways that friction is not useful**

Friction between the tyre and the road wears away the tyre.

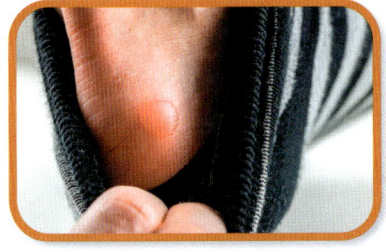

Friction between a shoe and your foot causes skin damage we call blisters.

Investigating scientific ideas

Revision topic 17 a/b

Here are some key points for this topic.

- Change only one variable in an investigation.
- Observe or measure the effect of the change to obtain your results.
- All other variables should be controlled to make a fair test or fair comparison.

- Repeat measurements to improve the reliability of your results.
- More reliable results mean that you can be more confident that you are making the correct conclusions.

- Look at measuring equipment carefully, at eye level, to read it more accurately.
- Measuring equipment has a scale and this has a unit.
- An accurate measurement is one that is as close as it can be to the real measurement.

When planning an investigation, write about keeping the volume of a liquid or the mass of a solid the same.

Avoid writing 'the same amount' for either of them.

Topic 7 | Revision

Here are some key things to understand and to be able to do.

■ **Identify questions that can be answered by doing an investigation and those that cannot**

> Think of two questions that can be answered by doing an investigation.

> Now think of two that cannot.

■ **Suggest questions to test scientific ideas and think of evidence that is needed to answer them**

> Discuss with a partner the evidence you need to answer your two scientific questions.

■ **Plan simple investigations by choosing the best equipment to use and how you will use it**

> Now discuss the equipment you will need for your investigations.

> How will you make them fair tests?

> Make sure you can name and draw equipment too.

Conclusions and evaluation of evidence

Revision topic 17 c/d/e

Here are some key points for this topic.

- Scientists collect evidence to answer scientific questions.
- Evidence may be observations, measurements or both.
- You use a results table to record data.
- Put the variable you change in the first column; write units in the column headings only.

- Results may also be presented as a key, a scatter graph, a bar chart or a line graph.
- Results are used to make conclusions.
- The pattern of a set of results can be used to predict new values.
- Results can be used as evidence to support a conclusion or to show that the conclusion is not supported.

Here are some key things to understand and to be able to do.

■ **Describe patterns in results and predict new values**

Scientific question: How does water temperature affect the number of bubbles of gas a pond plant makes?

Water temperature in °C	Number of bubbles counted in 1 minute
10	4
15	10
25	31

Predict how many bubbles will be made in one minute at 20 °C.

Decide which numbers it will be between.

Will it be 11?

Will it be 30?

Why not?

Describe the pattern the results show.

■ **Identify evidence that supports a conclusion**

A learner says that the results show that lots of bubbles make water hotter. Why is she **incorrect**?

■ **Suggest ways in which investigations can be improved**

How many times does the learner count bubbles?

Are her results reliable?

Did she collect enough data to plot a graph?

■ **Point out data that does not fit the pattern and suggest reasons why**

At 12 °C, the learner counts 11 bubbles in 1 minute.

This does not fit the pattern. What should she do?

She thinks that at 12 °C she didn't time one minute accurately.

Did she count for too long or not long enough?

End of topic questions

Revision

With a partner, look at the pictures of science equipment on the page opposite. Take turns to:

- name each piece of equipment; use the list below for help if you need it
- say what each piece of equipment is used for
- say the unit for any pieces of measuring equipment and how you write it.

circuit components	filter paper	stopwatch
Bunsen burner	test tubes	thermometer
measuring cylinder	ruler	magnet
filter funnel	scales (top pan balance)	force meter
evaporating dish	beaker	sieve

Topic 7 | End of topic questions

(key: b-bottom, c-centre, l-left, r-right, t-top)

Non-Prominent Image Credit(s):

123RF GB LIMITED: Anton Starikov 126 L-R 2b, 148 L T-B 2, berlinimpressions 11 T-B 2, boyenigma 119 L-R 2c, Darren Pullman 29 L-R 3c, gajus 143 L-R 1b, Marjorie A. Bull 35t, Nagy-Bagoly Arpad 6c, prensis 34t, suradech sribuanoy 131 L-R 1b, 68 L-R 2t; **Alamy Images:** Agencja Fotograficzna Caro 98 L-R 1c, Berndt Weissenbacher/BeKaHaWe 35c, Gina Kelly 118 L-R 2b, history_docu_photo 4, Keystone Press 16t, Nigel Cattlin 27b, Sciencephotos 63t; **GETTY IMAGES INCORPORATED:** Science & Society Picture Library 5t, ExperienceInteriors 37, laymul 82t, 82b, 84c, blueringmedia 118 L-R 2c; **Pearson Education:** Arvind Singh Negi/Red Reef Design Studio 106 L-R 2b, 135c, Clip Art Library 82, Coleman Yuen 148 L T-B 1, 61 T-B 4, Joey Chan 5b, Mohammed Ali 133, 148, 57c, 66c, 99t, Mohd Suhail 148 R T-B 1, 148 R T-B 4, 30 L-R 1c, 30 L-R 2c, 30b, 38, 64 L-R 1b, 64 L-R 1c, 64 L-R 2c, 86, Oxford Designers & Illustrators Ltd 107b, 135t, 143 L-R 1t, 143 L-R 2t, 52c, 57 L-R 2b, 86b, PDQ Digital Media Solutions Ltd 117 L-R 1t, 119 L-R 2t, 137b, 137c, 139b, 148 L T-B 4, 148 R T-B 3, 86 L-R 1t, 86 L-R 2t, Pearson Education Ltd 125t, 148, 45, 53b, 53t, 67, 74c, 76, 77, 81b, 90 L-R 1c, 90 L-R 2c, Studio 8 85 L-R 1t, Trevor Clifford 74 L-R 2b, Tsz-shan Kwok 102c, 86c; Utsav Academy and Art Studio 119 L-R 1t; **SCIENCE PHOTO LIBRARY:** ANDREW LAMBERT PHOTOGRAPHY 85c, MARTYN F. CHILLMAID 89c, SCIENCE PHOTO LIBRARY 85 L-R 2t, ST MARY'S HOSPITAL MEDICAL SCHOOL 17, TREVOR CLIFFORD PHOTOGRAPHY 61 T-B 1, 61 T-B 2, 61 T-B 3, 61 T-B 5; **SHUTTERSTOCK:** 5 second Studio 68 L-R 1b, 543709 83t, A Daily Odyssey 29 L T-B 1t, aappp 78, aelitta 118 L-R 1c, Africa Studio 110, 39t, 68 L-R 1t, akarlas 64 L-R 2b, Al More 23c, AlessandroZocc 28 L-R 1b, Alexander Raths 16b, Alexey Martynov 50c, Ali DM 48, All_White Background 39b, Anastasiia Skorobogatova 115 R T-B 2b, anat chant 22c, andriano.cz 3, Andrii Bezvershenko 7c, Andrii Symonenko 148 C T-B 5, angellodeco 2, Anna Jurkovska 8 L-R 2b, ANNA ZASIMOVA 136 L-R 2t, Arnain 119 L-R 3b, Artur Didyk 94, Artur Synenko 136 L-R 3t, 69 L-R 2t, atiger 34b, AVS-Images 96, Barks 49, Bess Hamitii 28 L-R 2b, Bildagentur Zoonar GmbH 64 L-R 2t, Birgit Reitz-Hofmann 14 L-R 2t, Blamb 38, BlueRingMedia 59b, 74 L-R 1b, 74c, BNP Design Studio 50b, Car n food designer 90b, carroteater 7b, ChWeiss 29 L-R 2c, Claudio Baldini 54, CobraCZ 59 L-R 2c, 59t, Creatus 143 L-R 1c, 89 T-B 1t, Cyrustr 35b, DImin 141t, dabjola 29 L-R 1c, Daisy Daisy 120 L-R 3b, Dan Boonjong 115 L T-B 1b, DariaBumblebee 75b, 75t, Denny Davidson 141c, Designua 131c, 24c, 67, Dragon Images 121 L-R 3t, Ekramar 131 L-R 3b, 71, Electrical Engineer 102c, epsylon_lyrae 119 L-R 3c, Erkki Makkonen 115 L-R 2t, Ethan Daniels 29b, Evgeniy Gromov 69 L-R 3b, FabrikaSimf 121 L-R 2t, Fedorov Ivan Sergeevich 148 L T-B 3, 85b, fen deneyim 132c, foto.grafs 134 L-R 2b, FrameAngel 136 L-R 5t, Gamzova Olga 55, gan chaonan 9 L-R 1t, Gear Digital 83b, George Schmiesing 29 R 1t, Gotta Studio 127 L-R 2t, graja 92t, GraphicsRF.com 102c, 33, 44, 99 L-R 1c, Gummy Bear 58c, gwolters 121 L-R 2c, 12c, 69 L-R 1t, Haoka 132t, Havryliuk-Kharzhevska 117 L-R 4b, Hennadii H 14 L-R 4b, huntingSHARK 98t, igor.kramar.shots 115 L-R 1t, Imageman 22b, Intarapong 89 T-B 3t, Irina Rostokina 121 L-R 3c, 13t, irishka5 29 L T-B 2t, Iurii Osadchi 95c, Jenson 89 T-B 2t, Jerry Gantar 21b, JKIWA 98c, jpreat 69 L-R 1b, Julio Salgado 26c, JungleOutThere 106 L-R 1b, Karamelity 70 L-R 1c, kaschibo 92 L-R 2c, Katia Titova 8 L-R 3b, Katrien Francois 20b, 24t, Kazakova Maryia 28t, Ketmanee 58b, 59 L-R 1c, kolessl 111, KonstantinChristian 126 L-R 1b, koosen 127 L-R 1c, Kopirin 14 L-R 3b, Kuttelvaserova Stuchelova 11 T-B 1, Lane V. Erickson 88 L-R 1b, Lia_Russy 14 L-R 1b, Lifestyle Travel Photo 136 L-R 1c, LightField Studios 127 L-R 3b, Lisa-S 121 L-R 1t, 8t, LumenSt 9 L-R 1b, Lydia Vero 121 L-R 1b, 13c, m.malinika 15 L-R 1t, 15 L-R 2t, 15b, 15b, Madlen 57 L-R 2t, Magic mine 36, Marcos Mesa Sam Wordley 111, Marek Hajdukiewicz 121 L-R 2b, 13b, Margo Harrison 91 L-R 1t, Marie Shark 32 L-R 1c, Marlon Lopez MMGI Design 39c, matuska 121 L-R 4b, 14c, mbarredo 119 L-R 4b, MeKaDesign 46b, 46t, mentalmind 60 L-R 1t, Microstocker.Pro 9 L-R 2t, mihalec 148 R T-B 2, Milosz_G 79, Modvector 127 L-R 2b, 62 T-B 1b, MriMan 32 L-R 2c, myboys.me 97, Mykola Mazuryk 136 L-R 4t, Nadezhda Nesterova 20t, nektofadeev 119 L-R 1c, Net Vector 130b, 65b, New Africa 131t, 60 L-R 2t, Nikola Bilic 58t, NOPPHARAT539 27t, Nowwy Jirawat 70 L-R 2c, Nungning20 57 L-R 1t, nyker 26b, Oleg Elkov 131 L-R 2b, 68 L-R 2b, Olga Aniven 143 L-R 2c, 88 L-R 2b, Olga_Narcissa 65 L-R 2t, Ondrej Prosicky 18, OneSideProFoto 120 L-R 1b, 6b, oriontrail 32t, Pabkov 120 L-R 2b, 8 L-R 1b, Pedro Monteiro 91 L-R 1c, Peter Kotoff 88t, petrroudny43 130b, 65b, picmedical 48b, Pineapple studio 127 L-R 2c, ppl 115c, PRILL 148 C T-B 2, redknapper 148 C T-B 3, renklerin kafasi 136c, RHJPhtotos 9 L-R 3t, Ropsie Chids 57 L-R 1b, Rostislav Stefanek 119 L-R 1b, Rsplaneta 42t, S_Photo 64 L-R 1t, Sandra Standbridge 20c, santanu maity 34c, sarin nana 119 L-R 2b, Scharfsinn 91 L-R 2t, Science Photo Library 148 L T-B 5, Siberian Art 141b, simonidadj 121 L-R 1c, 12b, Socialtruant 143 R T-B 1b, SOMMAI 115 L T-B 2b, Steve Allen 92 L-R 1c, TA BLUE Capture 41t, TamuT 9c, Tanja Esser 95t, tawanroong 121 L-R 3b, 14 L-R 1t, Th_Gim 69 L-R 2b, totojang1977 148 C T-B 1, tpfeller 127 L-R 1t, tr3gin 115 R T-B 1b, Tyler Olson 9 L-R 2b, Vaclav Sebek 119 L-R 3t, VASYL MIROSHNYCHENKO 91 L-R 2c, Vecton 38, Vector Tradition 134 L-R 1b, vectorlab2D 143 R T-B 2b, VectorMine 40t, 51, Vectorpocket 14 L-R 2b, Victor Josan 40b, vilax 127 L-R 3t, WAYHOME studio 42b, xpixel 127 L-R 1b, 62 T-B 2b, yusufdemirci 80c, 81t, Zmrzlinar 19.

All other images © Pearson Education